AN HOUR-GLASS ON
THE RUN

AN HOUR-GLASS ON
THE RUN

ALLAN JOBSON

And what is Life?—An hour-glass on the run,
A mist retreating from the morning sun,
A busy, bustling, still repeated dream.
JOHN CLARE

LONDON
ROBERT HALE & COMPANY

ISBN 0 7091 4860 7

Robert Hale & Company
63 Old Brompton Road
London SW7

16 12

Printed in Great Britain by
Lowe & Brydone (Printers) Ltd., Thetford, Norfolk

PREFACE TO THIS EDITION

Hour after hour, and day to day succeeds;
Till every clod and deep-drawn furrow spreads
To crumbling mould; a level surface clear,
And strew'd with corn to crown the rising year;
And o'er the whole Giles once transverse again,
In earth's wide bosom buries up the grain.

Bloomfield

◇◇◇

THE plot of ground in which my grandfather and his fathers lie buried is closed. It is as well for his long era has ceased and his day spent. His name, his lineage spanning the centuries, was of Suffolk, as were those of his neighbours. He lived in an unchanging world, season succeeding season, and could exclaim with Bloomfield year by year:

For every barn is fill'd, and harvest *done*!

The Industrial Revolution had touched his village and his life but little, although from a blacksmith's birth had sprung up an engineering works at Leiston, producing agricultural machinery, even traction engines that passed by his window. Then, on a clear day he could hear the trains streaking across his countryside to the west, the railroad of which he could remember being built. The day ending with sunset, he would give thanks to his God and retire to rest in an old four-poster hung with curtains and valance that had been the resting place of other generations before it became his own. His sleep would be untroubled until the break of another day.

There was one significant change that he had witnessed, when the plough team of oxen with their wide wooden yokes, gave way to the horse; the Suffolk Punch, bred by an old Suffolk farmer at nearby Ufford. Even so, the pace of life was not altered, it was an ambling leisurely trot, governed by a natural rather than a mechanical progress.

The horse in those peaceful years was everything to them, their one means of communication with the outside world, other than Shank's pony. The book next the Bible in many an old Suffolk farmer's home, and as large, was the Stud Book. Think of the trappings those lovely old creatures called into being; the wheelwright's yard, the blacksmith's forge, the harness maker's shop, the wayside inn and the ostler's bell. Even the carriage-builder, whose work shone like a spring morning. All these have vanished from the scene, gone with the wind of change. Yet the modern mind turns wistfully back to a peace it never knew. True, the outward show of that tranquil life is being preserved in museums like that at Stowmarket, although the spirit has fled. They are excellent in their way but the ethos is not there. They are for all the world like the Elgin Marbles, trophies of a tourist's excursion into yesterday's memories.

Those old Suffolkers were individualists from birth, especially the horse dealers, who had an answer to every question. A local yeoman was looking for a mount and introduced to one of these gentlemen who had what he thought would do. The animal was duly trotted out for inspection, so he started by asking about its pedigree. 'Well, that's like this here, its sire was a blood horse named Prepared, and its dam was a half-way mare' (i.e., half a cart horse and half a blood horse).

'Oh, well, that sounds alright, but my neck is worth something and I want a horse that will give me a day's hunting when I can find the time. Can he jump?'

'To be sure,' replied the seller; 'you see that gate down the yard, just put him at it!' The would-be purchaser did as he was bid and sailed over like a pheasant, returning in like manner.

'Yes, that's not bad,' said the jumper, 'but will he get me out of a mess if I get landed in one?'

'Do you know, Sir,' said the old coper, 'if he should land

you in hell overnight, he'll bring you out of it in the morning.' With that the chestnut changed hands, realising the sire was well named.

It is really remarkable how an old postcard album can bring back the past in a most vivid manner. In turning over the pages recently I came across two early pictures of the old Walberswick chain ferry that used to ply from bank to bank across the Blyth, both of which were taken from Blackshore quay on the Southwold side. The ramshackle craft is referred to on one of them as a pontoon.

Walberswick was the haunt of artists and art students, being described as 'quaint' in the language of those days. One of its claims to the picturesque was the bridges, rustic-like, that spanned the dykes of the salt marshes. They must have figured in many a sketch or amateur portfolio. But it was the pier and the sea shore that fascinated Wilson Steer when he tried so successfully to fasten the dancing light on to some of his pictures.

It was the message on the second card that set my mind back to earlier days, because it was addressed to 'Mr John Barham, Manor House, Middleton, nr Yoxford.' And was posted at Southwold. It reads: 'Dear Sir. I shall be at yours on Wednesday next all being well. Edward Sewell.'

To the ordinary person that would mean nothing, but I happen to know its significance. It goes right back to the proud days of the Suffolk Punch, that grand horse, so beautiful and docile an animal that looked its best when the sun shone on its sorrel coat, because Mr Sewell used to travel an entire horse from one farm to another. I can remember him so very well when he used to come on his visits to Middleton and I happened to be there. He would have two eggs for tea and stayed the night. I rather envied him those lovely eggs and probably 'eyed them wishly', as they used to say, because I had a good appetite, and new-laid farm eggs were something to remember. When you went to buy them at the dairy door, you would get 13 for 12 and each one would be done up separately in a bit of paper to keep them safe from breaking.

Now Mr Sewell, who was evidently a friend of grand-father's, followed a very old vocation. He would have started out on a Monday morning, possibly driving a little pony cart at a walking pace, the stallion roped on behind. I should hardly think he walked all the way himself.

But there is a little more in the card than that, because in all probability on that April morning so long ago now, when King Edward VII was on the throne and the squire still reigned supreme in the village and kept his parkland in such lovely trim, Mr Sewell would have crossed from Southwold on that old pontoon. It was miles nearer that way than coming round by the road. The countryside would have been on tip-toe for another spring and the cuckoo calling because

> In May—'a pipes all day,
> In June—'a changes 'as tune.

I wonder what the two men talked about after tea, sitting by the soft light of an oil lamp before a bright coal fire; and did Mr Sewell smell of horse? Old days when farming was in its prime? The present state of the market? And what the world was coming to? However, they were nine years away from Armageddon and in any case grandfather would not see it. Neither would they have realised that in a few years the horse would be superseded by the spluttering, smelly engines that had begun to run about the old roads. Fancy a Suffolk farm without a Suffolk horse, or a Suffolk road without the sound of a ring of iron on its dusty surface. However, it is good to think that even to this day one of the chief attractions of the Suffolk Show is when the Suffolk horses come on parade.

It is curious how the throb of life seems to keep pace with the speed created by man's mechanical inventions. Even the old horse-drawn coaches liked to emphasise their capabilities. Then came the railways when it was possible to go to London and back in a day from Ipswich. This was something the old folks never dreamed of when they went from Saxmundham *Bell* to the *Four Swans*, Bishopsgate or the *Bull* at Aldgate; or by waggon driven by S. Noller, a good old Suffolk name, to the *Blue Boar* at Aldgate on Tuesdays and Thursdays. Even so, time was of little consequence and folks had some in which they could stare. Now we have arrived at the jet-age, the most ordinary people become agitated by it and haven't got a moment to spare. This frenzied way of life has even entered into farming and the Suffolk fields. The change there is to say the least, phenomenal, for after all Suffolk is essentially an agricultural county, with soil which our Saxon forefathers knew how to value. Who could have visualised factory farming and the prairie-like outlook?

Everything has changed, even the horse pond that never dried up. The hedger and the ditcher have disappeared with the sweet-smelling overgrown borders of our acres. No longer does the cockerel crow at dawn and soon there will be no free-range eggs. The golden stacks in the stackyard no longer shine and harvest home is but a memory.

There are the remnants of a farm where I live, carried on in the old way by a man who has farming in his blood and cannot live without it. His kind heart is reflected in his stock. His old buildings are almost a ruin. I could not help re-marking to him that when his heritage goes, not only a bit of old Suffolk, but a bit of old England will go with it. A rather sad thought, but unfortunately true. Much of this headlong speed and artificiality has come about since the last war. This creates the necessity of a warning lest the industrial epoch destroy itself and ourselves with it.

These pages therefore can but serve as a Window on Yesterday.

CONTENTS

Preface to this Edition 5

Sweet Auburn 17

An Hour-Glass on the Run 30

Parent of the Blissful Hour 47

The Shelter'd Cot, the Cultivated Farm 59

Pastoral Symphony 75

The Cool Brick Floor 88

Thus, Thus, and Thus, We Compass Round 100

Village Companies 116

Country Characters 127

The Squire and His Relations 146

Old Cures 150

Country Calendar 158

Old Christmas 170

Rhyming Signs 178

Old Romance 182

ILLUSTRATIONS

Middleton Church	*facing page* 48
The Mill, Middleton	48
Carting from the field	49
Thrashing in the Stowmarket area	49
A giant has fallen	64
Beating the bounds at Hasketon or Burgh, c. 1888	64
The Middleton band	65
Bradfield St. Clare, about 1880	65
Cockfield Hall, Suffolk	112
Yoxford, Suffolk	112
A company of quoit players	113
Outside 'The Bull,' Bacton, nr. Stowmarket	113
A performing bear (1869)	128
Harvest men at Poplar Farm	129
Shooting party with gamekeepers and brushers	129

To Marian Lucy
just one year old

SWEET AUBURN

'. . . and at last we got into a real country road again, with windmills, rickyards, milestones, farmers' waggons, scents of old hay, swinging signs and horse troughs; trees, fields and hedgerows. It was delightful . . . and when a waggon with a train of beautiful horses furnished with red trappings and clear-sounding bells, came by with its music, I believe we could all three have sung to the bells, so cheerful were the influences around.'

Bleak House

❖◇❖

THERE is a spot in Suffolk which fills me with a quiet, comfortable pleasure every time I go near it. It is over sixty years since I first consciously saw it with the eyes of a three-year-old child, before even reason and judgement had developed; and as it thrilled me then so all through those eventful, strange years that lie between and which cover my life, the picture and the fragrance never fails. I smell again the faint perfume of the luxuriant nettle beds, catch the golden spread of the buttercups on Parson's Meadow, drink the sun-extracted fragrance of the box borders of the little sanded paths that led to my grandparents' door, hear the lark singing and see the white road that went up and over the hill into the wide spreading sky.

That spot to me was everything that could be visualised in the phrase, 'the English Countryside.' Beauty of spreading field and tumbling sky of gentian blue, smell, serenity, brooding peace, and a sense of far-offness; exercising a delicate interplay of emotions, so that I never catch one of those evanescent smells without being slipped back to those enchanting moments. Surely it was not long since those Elizabethan builders built that cottage which was my grandfather's home, fenced the garden with a flint wall, made the cart shed with the granary above, and adzed the timbers for the barn; while country folk (not unlike my grandparents) looked out through that same horn-like glass set in the leaded casements to see who was passing along the dusty road. Of course that was only yesterday, for time moved gently here, and the ways and doings of both my grandparents were Elizabethan by inheritance. There was hardly a job of any kind in the economy of that quiet household that was not carried out in the tradition of a long, long yesterday, and only in such manner well done.

The village is called Middleton-cum-Fordley, for it consisted of two parishes with two churches in one churchyard; and my grandfather's name was Barham. There were a large number of Barhams in the village, all extremely poor, related to one another, and all honourable in their transactions; but now not one remains. Grandmother's name was Brown, one of those ubiquitous Browns, common to almost every county, vying with the Smiths in number, and as English as the gardens they cultivated. But as she used to say, in the Great Day the names written in the Lamb's Book of Life would be neither Barham nor Brown but those given to them at the font. It was said—and rumours of that nature seem common in the circumstance—that through her came the blue blood. In any case she was gentle, if complaining, yet a true helpmeet. Certainly the name of Barham was honourable, with some pretensions to a county yeomanry background, originating in the adjacent village of Yoxford, and there recorded by a patrician gentleman who dealt in genealogies. But no one could go further back than the second generation, since their grandfathers stood at the root of their family tree.

Reverting to the name of the village, those who deal in place-names will know that there are a large number in England ending in 'ton.' This ending signifies several things, it may be a lofty site, an enclosure or homestead, or somewhere marked by a distinguishing feature, such as a tree, a hill, or even marshy ground. Since in this instance Middleton is low lying, the first must be ruled out, so we are driven back on the other two, of which you may take your choice. Trees abound, though none of great age, and there are also marshes adding their wistful beauty to the scene. You can find such flowers as meadow saffron, toadflax, chicory, marsh orchids (*alias* cuckoos in Suffolk), lady's bedstraw, the Roman nettle, and as one got near the sea, the bloody cranes-bill. But I like to think that this Middleton where my grand-parents lived was a homestead, so named in those far-off days by Saxon ancestors, who landing on that crumbling coast (some distance off then, but now within sound of the sea's roar), made their way inland and found this spot mid-way between that temperamental sea and the unknown beyond. In any case shards of Romano-British pottery have been found near the little river away in the marshes where a culvert connects two meadows.

My grandparents' old homestead was, and is, called Rackford Farm. Here again is subject for speculation, since it is quite near the fording-place of a little river known in the county as a splash. This shallow, pebbly bed of the stream allowing a foothold evidently accounts for the roadway, which I have no doubt is a Peddars' Way, since it can be traced northwards in a loke, or pathway, named Black Slough, which led past an ancient windmill and on to the once capital city of the East Anglian kingdom, Dunwich; and south past the gable-end of the manor-house, into a sunken lane known as the Wash, and on by the Packway Farm, soon after which it is lost. So then, Rackford may be a corruption of Trackway, or, according to some, have nothing to do with the Way itself but refer to a plant in the stream known as wrack. This may well be if you allow that Lackford in this same old county derives its name from the place where leeks were grown.

From which you will gather that Rackford Farm stands beside this old Peddars' Way, which may have led on to

Camulodunum, even to Londinium. That once it had a certain amount of importance, before it was folded up and put to sleep in an out-of-the-way corner of a wistful, willow-swept England.

The fields had names, alive and lovely, when grandmother picked cowslips to make her wine, or looked out from her tiny bedroom casements on to the harvesting crops. There was, for instance, the gentle slope adjoining the Drift leading up to the Ashen Yards. It was known as Mary's Acre. One wonders now if it merely commemorated some blowsy dairymaid, or whether it was the last remnant of a pious bequest, designed to light a candle before the shrine of the Queen of Heaven, when the village church was served by priests from the nearby abbey. However, the Bees' Pightle was instinct with sweetness and mead and metheglyn, as Gallows Hill with retribution and a swinging corpse. East and West Maypole were redolent of Merry England and the days when grandmother was young, when they danced on the lawn before Theberton Hall to the strains of a flute played by Ezekiel Elmey. But what of Grave Field and Hanging Grave? Were these the last resting-places of suicides? Certainly this was the case with Sarah Cobbler's Pit, since Sarah could hardly have been a cobbler in her own right. If she was then she must have been the first and last of her kind, for I have never heard of a woman cobbler. And here was her ghost.

Incidentally, Sarah Cobbler's Pit was along the Back Road Hill, and in its bosky depths spring by leafy spring grew the earliest primroses. Village children would vie with one another as to who could gather the first bunch. Times have changed and the pit is no more, for it has been filled in with local rubbish, collected from cottage gates by the local sanitary authorities; and Sarah's ghost has been laid.

The village was traversed by a number of footpaths, then

in constant use. They led to farmhouses, or cut off corners, but now their whereabouts are almost forgotten, and certainly their original use, say to a dairy door for milk and butter, has long since passed. One quite close to grandmother's front gate led just under the gable end of the manor-house, as already stated. One entered by a stile at the apex of a three-cornered plot in front of the barn and the house, made one's way by an old hedge and came out by a double dweller that stood by a hair-pin bend. It may have been—who knows?— the one for which Robert de Scales sought and obtained a licence 'to enclose a way leading from the highway beneath his dwelling-house in Middleton, towards the south, on providing another way.' It would be interesting to know where he lived, for I'll swear his house still stands somewhere in the village; and it would be still more interesting to know which pernickety twist in the road is to be traced to his tergiversation. But then it is a long time ago since Richard le Scot of Dunwich had free warren in this village; since Augustus, son of de Donewyco, claimed view of frankpledge and assize of bread and beer here; or Juliana, late wife of Richard Attemede, sued the Abbot of Leystone, etc., touching a tenement here; or lands were held by Robert de Scales, as of the Honor of Boulogne by knight service.

The oldest thing in the village was the church, part Norman, part Early English. At one time there were two churches in the one churchyard, and it is said that a fine linden tree marks the spot of the other church which was demolished. Which of the two was the older, I cannot say, but as the one that remains dates from Norman times that is long enough ago. But the truth is, this was a religious neighbourhood, and a large number of ruins testify to this fact. Civilisation and religion came to these parts in quite early times by reason of its proximity to the coast, and particularly so since the first bishop's see was so near. It is an interesting speculation as to whether this first Bishop Felix came so far as this

Middleton, in which case we can picture him making his way across Westleton Heath, one of his acolytes ringing a small handbell of primitive construction (merely four sheets of iron bolted together, or a single piece bent into a curve, and riveted down the sides), to announce his mission. Perhaps someone here was sick, in which case the bell would be rung before the Host, as he came on his way.

Whereas in some districts it had been necessary to create ruins in order to comply with the cultured taste born of the Grand Tour, and in fact became a craze when Capability Brown was landscaping the country, here in grandfather's county they were ready to hand. The horizon and the outlying fields were dotted with them, and you might have a chantry chapel in your own farmyard. Needless to say the natives thought nothing of them, and when one looks back and considers the years of neglect (fortunately it was mere neglect and not destruction), it is surprising they ever survived. Presumably it was not thought worth while even to use them for road-making.

Near at hand were the ruins of the Franciscan monastery at Dunwich, and also the apsidal end of a Saxon Lazar chapel. Dominican or Black Friars had been here also, and a cell to the Order of St. Benedict at Eye, but these had been washed away. Then in the opposite direction, and the nearest to Rackford Farm, were the ruins of the Premonstratensian Abbey at Leiston, which had been founded in 1183 by Ranulph de Glanville near the sea, where a ruined chapel still stands. It was removed to its present site in 1363, so that, of course, was quite recent. Sibton, only just through Yoxford, held the ruins of a Cistercian Abbey of the White or Grey Monks, the only one in the county. Since these brothers preferred wild and uncultivated districts you may be sure that Sibton was on the edge of beyond.

Butley, by the way, held a magnificent achievement of arms in another stately ruin, founded again by our Ranulph de Glanville. But then Butley was also known by its pub, which was the 'Oyster,' and oyster patties in grandmother's time were no mean delicacy. Perhaps the recipe came out of that priory kitchen.

The Augustinians had ruins at Snape, Orford and also Blythburgh, while Campsey Ash had once housed their nuns; and more Franciscan nuns, who only had but three houses in the whole country, had one at Bruisyard.

So antiquity was in every field. Legends, secret passages, strange happenings, portents and fears abounded. For example, it was said, and as certainly believed, that if you were born in the Chime Hours you could hear music in the ruins of Leiston Abbey; but if you should go to investigate then the music would stop, to begin again as you drew away. (Eliza, who was the more romantic of grandmother's two elder girls, wanted to know if the sounds came from a silver organ, but Rebecca, her sister, said no, it was a barrel organ, the same as they had at church. Eliza maintained that only a silver organ could give out elfin music.) Then, too, there was an underground passage here which led to Framlingham Castle; but you must keep out of that at all costs, for if you were to venture inside you would never be able to get out again! Since no one knew where that entrance was it didn't seem to matter much. Perhaps it was done to frighten the children and keep them within bounds.

But some were not mere legends since they were historic facts, as that connected with Cockfield Hall, Yoxford, the old portion of which had served as a prison for poor unfortunate Lady Catherine Grey, sister to Jane. Her bedroom was still there having become one of the apartments of the house-keeper. It looked out into a quiet secluded courtyard, flanked by a gem of a gatehouse, later acclaimed as a perfect speci-men of mediaeval brick.

When Catherine died, in that cold January of long ago, having been brought there the previous October, her body rested for a while in the village church. It is alleged that her poor little dog pined for her, and lay and died of grief on her temporary grave. Her body was eventually taken to Salisbury Cathedral, where she lies with her husband under a magnificent memorial. She had married without permission and was imprisoned for it. Amongst the heirlooms of that house was her chest, covered with Cordova leather, decorated with rustic scenes, banded with iron and fastened by great locks and decorated hasps.

If the ruins and certain trees were landmarks, certainly the village inns were waymarks; not only somewhere to bait your horse but a guide to the very few travellers. At Middleton was the *Bell*, thatched like the church, but at Kelsale it was the *Eight Bells*, so named from the fine peal in the nearby belfry, one of the prettiest for miles around. At Westleton stood the *Crown*, brick-fronted and covered with Gloire de Dijon roses; then at Darsham was the *Fox*. Yoxford had the *Three Tuns*, a posting-house, large and comfortable withal, with one of the finest bowling greens for miles around. But at Theberton they went into the *Lion*, obviously a reference to heraldry. And, of course, Dunwich had the *Ship*, since it was on the edge of the water; and here they not only brewed their own beer (as did the others), and put it into the nicest little stoneware bottles you ever saw, but gave their customers a biscuit to mumble with their beer. If this was not of monkish origin, then I don't know anything about it, for I would wager they were baked on wafer irons which you can see today in their little museum, exactly the same sort of iron as was used for making wafers for the celebration of the Mass. But now, what of outlandish Eastbridge? For, as grandmother used to say of a sister-in-law who was stupid enough to bury herself there, 'Once Eastbridge, always Eastbridge!' Well, they had a little low-lying pub there which they called the *Eel's Foot*; but then they were smugglers. Saxmundham had the *Angel*, and Sibton the *White Horse* to match their White Brothers. Needless to say, many if not all of these inns were of ecclesiastical origin, such as the *Fox and Goose* at Fressingfield, and the *Queen's Head* (not Victoria) at Dennington. And here, in this latter lovely old church, is the alabaster altar tomb of Sir William Phelip, who fought at Agincourt. He later became Lord Bardolph through his marriage with Joan, Lady Bardolph.

Let us for a moment go back to the river, which was full of eels and jack pike, for it provided the northern boundary of the village, dividing Middleton from its uncivilised neighbours at Westleton. It ambled on 'quietly through green level lands, so quietly, it knew their shape, their greenness and their shadows well.' And then it passed into the great North Sea by means of an old Dutch sluice. After all

> Even the weariest river
> Winds somewhere safe to sea.

The ford had been provided on the west side with a rickety plank bridge for the use of foot passengers, while vehicles used the splash. Here many a pitched battle had been fought between the two parishes, since they were rivals, the northern neighbours being adept at fighting and stone-throwing. On the opposite bank was a curious formation known as the Mumbery Hills. In high summer it was purple with heather, but in late autumn and winter it loomed grimly austere and utterly lonely. Beautiful in the long, late, rose-shadowed twilight, but forbidding when the grey skies betokened a tempest. Here in the hollows the nightjars answered to the owls' call; mystery deepening in winter when the Jack-o'-lantern (Peggy-with-a-lantern, Willy Wish, Jenny Lantern) danced across the wastes, leading those who were Will-led to destruction. One could watch them bobbing about in fiendish fashion, which was something neither grandfather nor his friends cared to see.

There was a path along the south bank all the way to the sea, so that one could note the

> . . . late fowl travel on the shadowy mere
> Towards her reedy island and her nest.

Then, as one neared the sea, after passing the old brick arch that once connected certain sheep-walks, one came to the shallow pools where dwelt the shelduck, redshanks, sandpipers, terns, godwits, ruffs, dunlin, and even the avocet; while that great lonely fisherman, the heron, would see you approach afar off, spread his wings and lollop slowly across the sky. Grandfather called him a harnser, and there was one of his tribe, stuffed and in a glass case, standing on the old chest of drawers in the parlour of Rackford Farm, silently, unwinkingly testifying to the prowess of grandfather and his gun.

Since grandfather lived by the soil, the most important thing to him was his weather-glass, which hung in the backhouse, suspended from the ceiling near the window. It consisted of a bottle filled with water, with an inverted flask stuck in its wide neck. Changes in the weather were denoted by the rise and fall of the water into the flask. But grandfather could read the sky almost as well as this barometer, and knew of coming changes by certain actions of his stock, particularly his pigs; and by the rooks in the sky. But after all, the moon ruled the weather and was a very real person to both grandparents. They watched its face and paid particular attention to the first moon of the year. Then again they watched the stars, especially those which 'whooly ran,' being careful to note the direction. If one ran to the right it meant good news, but if to the left, bad. There was, of course, the weather vane on the church spire; some said it had been there since the days of William the Conqueror; and it might have been as far as their time was concerned.

And there was another on the gable-end of the barn, a pretty thing wrought long years ago on the village anvil.

In their fruitful memory were recorded the vagaries of the atmosphere. They used to say as they wagged their heads and watched the corn sprouting,

> Under water, famine;
> Under snow, bread.

And

> If on Candlemas Day the thorn hangs a drop,
> Then you may be sure of a good pea crop.

Grandfather could just remember January 6, 1814, when it began to snow, and the frost continued until March 20th, so that a white world lasted for nigh on three months. And there was that year of omen, 1825, when wrecks were piled up along the coast in the January gales; and many a village lad was drowned. There was another memory in later years of the Crimean winter of 1855, when it began to freeze on February 1st, and did not give until March 15th. Then on Christmas morning, 1860, there was another great spell of cold, when many old trees were split by the frost. One in particular, in Theberton Park, a relic of imparking, had a bole of enormous girth with a great branching head. In grandfather's words—'Blaarm yar skull, bor, that fare tew break up like some owd bee-skep!'

But perhaps the greatest phenomenon of all was in November 1848, when there was an extraordinary display of the Aurora Borealis. Poor old Joe King (of whom grand-mother bought her milk in later years), looking out from his low cot and seeing that strange and lovely light, thought the village was on fire, including his little square-faced chapel; and that the world had come to an end.

> Fearful lights that never beacon
> Save when kings and heroes die.

The old church spire stood out, just topping a rise in the ground, the brazen cock on the weather-vane glittering like a fire bird limned against a burning sky, and folks said they could have seen to mend by the light it made.

A darkness made of too much day.

Grandmother's day started very early, almost at the crack of dawn, when all outward things stood in the sharp radiance of the first lovely light, and lasted to the late evening, when the shadows grew long. Her mornings were filled with house-wifely duties, but at evening she would sit by the fire either netting or sewing, often waiting for her husband who had 'gone down street'; or talking over with him the dear old times, the simple, kindly, primitive times of their youth. Grandfather was quite a bit older than grandmother, for when he was following the plough at the Valley Farm, having come up from scaring crows to that honourable position, he had seen grandmother coming to the dairy door for milk, carrying one of those shiny tin cans with a lid and a handle. He watched her more than once, all unbeknown to her, and said to himself, 'I'll marry her when she's growed up a bit.' And so he did, and they had lived happily ever afterwards. As far as grandfather was concerned, she was always that little bit of a gal he had first known, with her dark frizzy hair, lovely, elfish, almost violet eyes, with their shadowy depths, perfectly formed chin and teeth as white as blanched almonds. He had not forgotten her loveliness in profile and her little stiff manner in standing, and although now she was getting bent about the shoulders, felt the cold and dreaded the wind, yet she was to him the same little girl he had first known; his Susannah. (When I first knew her, the mildly wayward hair was drawn down tight and smooth, parted in the middle and just visible under her cap.)

The far-away tick of a clock, and the soft purr of the flames on the hearth would be the only sounds in her parlour, grandfather all but asleep in his great chair with wings, aflame in turkey twill. She would sew quietly with such tiny needles (Whitechapel sixes and Arnott's patent sewing cotton) by the light of two composite candles. Then let the work drop on her lap and sit quite still listening, perhaps to the wind in the great chimney that to her was so full of portent. This was the one hour which upgathers all the lost hours of the light as cast blossoms. Then she would nod sideways into her chair and fall asleep. Presently it would be—

'You know, John, I ha' jist had a funny owd dream!'

'Oh!'

'I dreamt the rectory was afire!'

'Oh!'

'Yes, an' they were a bringin' on the things out and putting them on the lawn.'

'Oh!'

'Then someone up an' say—"Let's have an auction!" '

'Oh!'

'And do you know, John, I bought that nice little old chaney tea set what Mrs. White think such a lot on.'

'Oh!'

'Don't keep on saying "Oh!" '

'No!'

'Nor "no" neither; for then I woke up.'

'Well, gal, that's just as well you did.'

'Yes, but I like drinking my tay out o' nice thin chaney cups; that fare to taste better.'

'Oh!'

'There you go again.'

'No!'

'But I do, so there.'

'Oh!'

AN HOUR-GLASS ON THE RUN

There I meet common thoughts, that all may read
Who love the quiet fields: . . .
That in some mossy cottage haply may
Be read and win the praise of humble tongues
In the green shadows of some after-day.   *John Clare*

◇◇◇

IN writing of the days of my grandparents there are one or two things which I should like to stress, since they belong to those times and have passed away so completely. The first was the lovely smell which was inherent in the hedge-rows draped in hawthorn and honeysuckle, and in the verges lined with huge docks, burdocks, teasels, hogweed and wild parsnip, to say nothing of campions, cornflowers and poppies. This was mixed with the gritty dust of the roads, the sweat of horses and Stockholm tar. Then there were the gardens. In grandmother's case, as you might expect, it was Elizabethan in character. Little sanded paths ran here and there between low box borders, like a knot garden, and rivalled one in fragrance and atmosphere. In high summer the hollyhocks grew so tall that they almost turned into the bedroom windows. And, of course, there was a fuchsia. When the sun shone on this it loosened a gentle perfume which lingers in the memory even now. Grandmother's neighbour, another Barham, was a gardener-coachman at the rectory, and he went in for pansies, which also were grown in little beds ringed with box. Other smells came from the stackyard, of hay and straw, and large beds of nettles. Then from the granary came mealy smells and that of oil-cake housed there. From the sties, the bullock yard and the stables, and not least the grease in the cart shed came other and more pungent smells. Something pleasant, even fragrant could be found about an empty sack.

Then, when one entered the cottage, it too was permeated

by a delicate sweetness penetrating every nook and cranny, of which there were plenty. Of course the linen was stored in lavender, southernwood and balm, as by ancient custom, but the smell of the garden came in by the open door, mixing itself with the coco-matting on the floor and the odour of apples to be found in the further bedroom. Even the clothes they wore were steeped with this smell of the fields and were as fragrant as a crofter's tweed. In all, it was a smell peculiar to the country, and when grandfather sent a parcel to one of his girls in London, it would be carefully sewn up in a clean unbleached linen wrapper, and the smell would travel with it. There was no mistaking whence it had come.

Of course there were other smells. Yes, I know, for the little sentry-box draped in ivy or elder which stood not too near the backhouse door wanted a bit of stomaching. It filled me with dread, although the seats were scrubbed as white as wood ash would allow, and the walls hung with pretty striped wall-paper, and the church almanac made gay the back of the door. As for the muck which they cromed up from the stackyard and spread on the fields, I have always rather enjoyed that. But I can assure you from personal memory that the lovely smells which were inherent in the countryside and part of it far outdid anything of disagreeableness. Alas! this lovely country quality has gone, overpowered by the petrol fumes.

Another quality, fittingly complementary to the other, was that of stillness. The air seemed still, as quiet as a mouse, so that what sounds there were travelled long distances and were full of music and echoes. The crunch of wheels grinding on the gritty road and the clip-clop of the horses. The barking of a dog (a portent at night) at some distant farmstead; the blare of a cow robbed of her calf; the bleating of sheep—and there were many flocks in those days. To these were added on market days the ring of bells on the horses, which beside the sound was as equally pretty a sight. Added up it was peace—the peace and quiet of a countryside which today, unfortunately, knows no such thing.

True, this peace spelt something of loneliness, for strangers were rarely seen, and if one should appear then he would be watched by many unseen eyes, and speculations made as to whence he had come and where bound. It was nothing uncommon for, say, Fred Vincent (Charlie Chambers's wife's mother's brother), to hold a conversation with a fellow labourer in the next field, an acre or so away. As for a passing trap, surely that demanded a hail and a wave of the cap! But it also developed a clannishness, a splendid isolationism, and a pride in one's own parish that held the best bell-ringers, the best quoit players, and the finest harvest men for miles around.

The only changes that came about in those apparently timeless years were those wrought by Time itself. Adding crannies to walls, mellowing old bricks, excoriating old oak, softening the outlines of barns and homesteads, even clothing old iron with a certain scaly beauty. And there was a simplicity of outlook with its attendant pleasures, and an infinite enjoyment in ordinary everyday things; walks across the fields, resting-places, turnstiles, extending even to Susan Barham's asthma and Keziah Brown's rheumatism. Old Wives' Tales were grandmother's Vanity Fair, and yesterday was so near.

Aunt Mahala, commenting on the modern trend, even then becoming apparent, and deploring constant change, had a favourite text she was always quoting; it was, 'Whose strength is to sit still.' As she was so prone to say, wagging her head, 'Fooks fare as though they can't, they're allus a betty-ing about arter suffen!' However, grandmother used to counter this sometimes with the remark, 'There's nothing like a glass o' cold water for hysterics.'

Grandmother was married when she was eighteen and her wedding dress hung in the closet next to the great chimney on the parlour chamber. Grandfather didn't know, but she knew, and sometimes all unbeknown to him she would have just a peep at this sprigged lilac gown which she had made herself, even to the hoops of briar thongs, peeled of their bark. There was a hat there too, which consisted of a funnel-like trumpet of straw, trimmed with faded ribbon, ruched round the front with now tousled lace, and lined with blue silk. She had only worn it that once, since she thought it a bit out of place, for it had come to her from the Hall; and she preferred to be herself and not be out of her station, even by the matter of a bonnet.

There was something else in that cupboard of sleeping memories, a box which contained a white shift, white stockings, white mittens, and a white lace cap. They were for her burying, waiting until she should need them, and the women would know where they were.

The Browns lived at Hog Corner, which is just by Valley Farm, while grandfather was then employed at the Moor Farm. It was a walking wedding, which was the usual custom, but it must have been a very pretty sight as the bridal party wended its way to the old church. Leaving their cottage home they turned in by the Valley Farm, skirted the sunken road, then known as the Wash (the old Peddars' Way), crossed the ten-acre diagonally and came on to Fletcher's Lane, and so to the church. This is a particularly beautiful part of the village, deep set as it were in the countryside, surrounded by many beautiful trees, having Theberton Park to the south-east, the Valley Farm in the hollow, and then the ground rising gently towards the north and the church. In the Spring Pond field is an ancient pond, the home of sundry water hen, and fringed with willows; a pond that has never been known to run dry even in the hottest summer. Curiously enough, a George I guinea, dated 1720, was but recently ploughed up in the field, obviously lying there when the bridal company passed, dropped by a farmer perhaps on his way to church, since no labourer could have possessed such a piece.

Needless to say, grandfather was waiting at his church, where his father and mother had been married before him. Even then showing signs of his choleric temperament, being all heated up lest something should go wrong.

After the return journey for a little festivity, the happy pair went straight to their new home, a cottage on the Moor; but shortly afterwards grandfather got the position of bailiff at Rackford Farm to which they removed and there he remained until after grandmother's death.

My grandmother had three girls and two boys, only one son reaching maturity, the other dying at a very early age. This was grandmother's first real grief, and that little turfed mound in the churchyard, spangled with primroses in spring time, was always in her thoughts. Upstairs in the drawer of a choice little toilet glass (how she had come by it no one seemed to know, but you can find the design today in Sheraton's *Book of Designs*), was a lock of his hair folded in a piece of white paper, and in another drawer were his marbles, by which he had set such store. The girls' names were, in proper order, Eliza, Rebecca and Susie; the last after grandmother and her favourite, but the diminutive was for her alone, since grandmother was and remained all her life unabridged Susannah. And the boy was Charles.

Not a large family, it is true, as families then went, but it stretched the family purse to breaking-point. This meant that in a very short space of time the children, as they had come, went out one by one. Eliza, the eldest, to her grandmother. Rebecca, the next, to her aunt who was childless; while the youngest remained at home. The boy left home as soon as he was old enough to learn a trade. How it came that the grandmother took Eliza, I cannot say, for she was a poor widow who eked out a livelihood by repairing sacks at a few coppers a score, and whose earthly possessions, or those that were of any value, would go into a wheelbarrow. It must have been a very temporary arrangement. The aunt, on the other hand, was better off, married to grandfather's brother, a splendid housekeeper, greatly skilled in all housewifely duties.

Poor as they all were, yet these children had what education there was, at a penny a week apiece, at a school in the village street kept by a Mrs. Davey, whose husband, a helpless sort of person, was addicted to snuff. This was all very well, but as soon as they could read (or was it taking arithmetic?) the fee was doubled. Twopence was certainly a lot of money, especially when two or three children from one household attended school, so that tuition soon came to an end. Since they were all chapel-goers, they attended the Sunday-school, where they were also taught the rudiments of learning, but considering the Class Leaders and the teachers had not much of learning themselves it is difficult to see how they could impart it to others. Great-aunt Rebecca, with her smiling face, was a teacher in that Sunday-school until she was over eighty.

The children made their own fun, as children will, ransacking the hedgerows for wild flowers and wasps' nests and grass snakes, sometimes finding as much as a saucerful of wild strawberries to take home. The number of little rhymes and tags which were always on their lips testify to their happiness. One can imagine them tripping across the footpaths, some from quite a long distance, picking violets but leaving the lords-and-ladies severely alone; their childish voices and laughter being carried on the wind—

> Blessed Bishop Barnabee,
> Tell me when my wedding be.
> If it be tomorrow day,
> Spread thy wings and fly away.

Mrs. Davey, the schoolmistress, wore a mob cap with

35

deckle edges, spectacles, and a merino gown, with a shawl pinned round her shoulders, and her cane lay very near to hand. The children learnt by memory, that being the only method, but they could all mend and put on patches, the girls could embroider and mark. Moreover they could knit, and even the boys could turn out a pair of stockings with ease. Evidently that was inherent in another little rhyme—

> Hold up your head,
> Turn out your toes,
> Speak when you're spoken to,
> Mend your clothes.

As some of the children came long distances they would bring their dinner in little lidded baskets, the food wrapped up in clean white napkins or perhaps tied up in a coloured handkerchief. If the weather was good they would eat it out of doors, if not, then in the schoolroom. Needless to say they found a good deal of enjoyment in exchanging certain tit-bits with one another, since Rebecca's mother's bread was much nicer than Mariah's, and as for Naomi's scraps, they were delicious. Although not large in numbers, they had their camps and clans, as is evidenced by one of their oft-repeated rhymes—

> Long and lanky,
> Black and proud;
> Fair and foolish,
> Little and loud.

Then there were games, some at guessing, such as the one of holding a pea-pod behind the back—

> Even or Odd?
> Pusket or Cod?

Since their boots were such an eternal problem, although they often won a new pair by their own efforts at gleaning—

> Tip at the toe, live to see woe.
> Wear at the side, live to be a bride.
> Wear at the ball, live to spend all.
> Wear at the heel, live to save a deal.

Some of the girls went to the church Sunday-school, and some to the chapel. The former were apt to look down on the latter, but the chapel sniffed its nose at the question and answer instilled into the church children—

> 'What is your duty to your neighbour?'
> 'To keep my hands from picking and stealing, and my tongue from evil speaking, lying and slandering!'

Needless to say, the boys would run after the girls, who professed to hate their attentions, particularly if the former had a piece of sassafras to stick down their necks—the 'horrid owd stuff!' The girls were dressed more or less alike, dark stuff dresses, worsted stockings, lace-up boots with fish-mouth tops, full of the most wonderful creases; and over all a pinafore. To all intents they were smaller editions of their mothers, who also invariably wore an apron, which they called a mantle, the Anglo-Saxon *mentel*. 'Where's my mantle?' she would exclaim in an emergency—a job of work, or for going down the street to shop, or for putting over her head, in case of annoyance or fright, or dealing with the bees. And she considered it an omen of ill-luck if the strings came undone of their own accord.

A boy's boots of the period were armour plated, with close rows of hobnails, and iron plates and tips, and the girls' boots could not have been much better. Even little children of two and three were provided with these miniature dreadnoughts, as unearthings at Women's Institutes have demonstrated. All hand-made by the village 'shummaker,' of which there were three in this small community, George Baldry, John Newson and William Rouse.

After sunset, the only light in those days (not so long ago, after all) was by means of rushlights and candles, both of which were made at home. Eliza, being the eldest, would gather the rushes from the marshes at the end of the stack-yard, peel them in the approved manner, that is leave a strip of the outer covering to act as a strengthener to the pith, and then they would be dipped in molten fat held in a roughly shaped pan designed for the purpose. Some of the humorous ones described them as fried straws, and the smell during the process must have ousted other and more fragrant odours. A good-sized rush would last an hour, and it was Eliza's job also to adjust this in the nip as it burned down. Candles were made in moulds, and if no metal ones could be found, then a length of dried cow-parsley stalk would be sought, cut between the knuckles, which made excellent moulds. The fat for the candles, as also for the rushlights, was saved for the purpose, and had as little salt in it as possible. The wicks were knitted by grandmother and then dipped in boracic to make them burn brightly and free from 'snaast.' It was not until their later years that grandfather and grandmother had the luxury of a paraffin oil lamp, since these did not come into general use until the 'seventies. Some of the better-off families had a colza-oil lamp that went by clockwork.

Neither were matches very common, although sticks of wood with sulphur tops could be had for a penny a bundle. One of grandmother's heirlooms, bequeathed to her by her mother, was a tinder box. In her younger days she would never go to bed without this, and a candle placed on a chair near to hand in case it should be wanted in the night. And there was always a word of advice that seemed to come up out of the grave, 'Git the owd tinder box ready for the morning, gal! and keep the lint and brimstone dry, else you'll repent it!' When things changed, grandmother kept her box on the mantelshelf as a reminder of the old days.

Sunday was always a bright day, the best day of the week. Certainly it meant Sunday-school and long, long services. Discipline in those days, even in Sunday-school, was no empty phrase. If you were not careful the superintendent, or one of the teachers, would lump on to you right hard, and if he couldn't reach you with his hand, would use a stick or a hymn book. However, there were hymns to sing and sometimes the sermons, even the prayers, were funny. Those who came long distances would bring their meals and camp out, using the chapel stove in winter to 'hot-up a bit of wittals.' Then, of course, at the Anniversary it meant something new to wear, since grandmother would run-up a bit of stuff if she possibly could.

Sunday, too, was different from the rest of the week, for in the evening the Bible would be brought out, and all would read round, grandfather first, then grandmother, Eliza, Rebecca, Susie and Charlie. Needless to say they travelled into strange places, from Dan to Beersheba, Jerusalem to Jericho, met very unusual people such as Parthians, Medes and Elamites, and often tripped over by the wayside owing to the difficulties of the terrain, and the limitation of a penny a week curriculum.

In the winter this reading round was done by the aid of a rushlight candle held in an ancient stick, as monks in choir used to do. This was handed round to each reader in turn, since the smelly light only gave sufficient illumination to see the darkness, but it sometimes meant singed eyelashes if they were not careful. Many of the Biblical proper names were, of course, alive to the children, for the village was peopled with prophets and seers who somehow looked their parts as they grew older and older and their hair turned white. And they were not all gloomy prophets, since many had a shining face, as I can just remember, made thus by their religion, since their earthly lot was not exactly heavenly. And the family would end up with a hymn that remained with them as a favourite all their days:

> Now the day is over,
> Night is drawing nigh,
> Shadows of the evening
> Fall across the sky.

Like all the other cottage homes, it was early to bed, for there was that other end, the beginning, which was also early. There were only two bedrooms in that cot, the further one leading off from the larger or parlour chamber. Charlie had to sleep in the closet, which was so full of other sleepers besides himself. The girls would crowd into the one little room, two girls into one truckle bed only large enough for one, and Liza on the floor. The moon would stream in through the tiny casement, and if they looked out all would be peace and quiet, save Boxer or Diamond chewing at his manger and giving an occasional stamp; and the great blue dark heaven arching over all, with the plough hanging, as it were, over the gable-end of the barn. Then, if eyes were not too heavy, sundry little bits of gossip would be exchanged. Susie would be full of fears and questioning, 'Liza, do you think Polly is a witch?'

'Hush, Susie, there's no such things these days,' from Becca.

'But she looks so queer with that squint o' hers. And do you know, Liza, I heard Mr. Spalding say to father that it was a funny old thing but his horses would never go past old Ninny Free's at night. And they say she's a witch an' can stop a team of horses just when she will!'

'Look you here,' said practical Eliza, 'don't you worry your head over witches and people like Polly and Ninny

Free, just before going to sleep. Don't you think Mrs. White rather nice? Folks say she finds it lonely at the rectory, and I think she likes you, Susie.'

'Yes, I do like her. She's the sort of lady I'd like to be when I grow up. Fancy all those lovely things, and that lovely garden, and unhappy. Isn't it funny?'

'No, Susie, it isn't really funny. P'raps it is because she hasn't got a little Susie herself! All those rooms and no children. That don't bear thinking about. Just think o' Mrs. Marjoram in that little old hovel, ten children and no husband!'

After this a silence, then, 'Liza, one of my ears ha' been tingling real bad today!'

'Oh, which one?'

'This one!'

'Well, I can't see in the dark. Don't you know left from right?'

'That's the one this side on the pillow.'

'That must be the right, then; well, that mean spite.'

'Do it now. What do that mean on the other side?'

'Oh, that mean love.'

'Coo!'

'An' if you think of a person who is likely to be talking about you, and mention the name aloud, the tingling will stop if you say the right one.'

'What a pity! I wouldn't know what name to say, so I couldn't find out. And I'd whooly like to know!'

Later on, 'I like Mrs. Doughty, don't you together?'

'Yes,' from both of the elders.

'Do you know? I heer'd say—'

'You ha' got some rare ears, Susie!'

'Yes, I know, I can't help that. I heer'd Susan talking to mother, an' she say Mrs. Doughty ha' never had a pair o' walking shoes all her life. Do you think that's true?'

'Why not? She ha' got that yalla carriage, so she don't

need to walk. But go you off to sleep, Susie, else you'll be late for school.'

'All right, but I'm glad I've got a good pair. I wish folks wouldn't call them highlows!'

Grandmother made grandfather's shirts, each of which took four yards of calico that cost threepence a yard. This was folded over like a sheet of paper to the length of the garment, not exactly in half, allowing the back to be longer than the front; and the calico was doubled, back to front, down to the bottom of the armpits. It was then sewn up the side, with gussets by the flaps, and gussets again at the neck. That is, the material was stitched to fit with the tucks rather than any should be cut away. The arms were put in square, and when the shirt was worn the shoulders fell away over the upper arm. This sounds a bit uncomfortable, but it gave ample room for movement. Sometimes she used tin buttons, quite flat, bought for a penny a dozen of Mary Mullinger at the door; but sometimes they were three-fold linen ones.

Grandfather's shirts were his most important undergarments, since he never wore vests and pants. As his trousers were always lined he seldom felt the cold, and it was always said they would stand up of their own accord, without legs in them; but they used to say that also of grandmother's worsted stockings that started life by being black, and then changed to green as the years rolled by! He usually wore a neckcloth that varied from turkey twill, striped material to plain white linen.

His trousers were fastened below the knees by a wisp of hay or a bootlace, the latter bearing the name of 'ligers, which was a corruption, presumably, of Elijahs. This gave greater freedom to the knees and was kinder to the trousers during work in the field; besides, it helped to keep the bottoms out of the wet. Black bone buttons were used, fastened on with wax thread, bought by the ounce, as in his opinion reel-thread was of no use. Later he complained that the new buttons, presumably meaning those made by machine, wore the thread to bits. In summer the heavy trousers were discarded and those of drabbet substituted, while the buttons, starting white, soon turned to a lovely ivory shade. This drabbet was strong stuff, and was used also for the smocks. An odd piece would be turned into a Long Melford purse, which was shaped like a modern tobacco pouch. All his trousers were fitted with a fob pocket to hold his turnip watch, which for safety's sake was also tied to his braces.

Besides making his shirts grandmother knitted his braces of white thread, with a cross-over at the back, and on the front straps were two or three button-holes to allow for adjustment. As there was no metal there were no iron marks to contend with. She knitted his garters as well.

Needless to say, grandfather had several shirts, but there was one in particular of which he was very proud. It was a splendid, ample creation of calico, made by his mother for his seventeenth birthday, and begun soon after his birth. Made like the others in cut it differed from them in having a series of pleats down the front. It served him for special occasions all his long life.

The old people were always careful about changing their clothes, especially the casting off of any garment, taking due note of the month, however hot the sun, calling to mind those who had been caught unawares:

> Beneath this little mound of clay
> Lies Captain Ephraim Daniels,
> Who chose the dangerous month of May
> To change his winter flannels.

Grandmother had her own way in dealing with chills, and grandfather's chest was the weakest part about him. It was bed for him if he came in a bit wheezy after having sat on the exposed seat of his pony cart, coming home in the wind and the rain, without lights, relying on his Jenny to pick a path. Then, on his hairy chest was placed a large and strong-smelling hot tallow brown-paper plaster! And it was of no use wriggling, for on it went, firmly and securely, only to come off with wear. He must have looked a funny sight, in nightshirt, tasselled nightcap, and with his face so red against the sheets and pillow-slips.

Grandmother was not one of those who always ran to the doctor. After all, he lived three good miles away, and, poor man, with the best intention in the world it was not always possible to come. But when he came it was with an air of robustness that would set one's mind at rest, a laugh and, 'Where's it hitting you, partner?' Besides, she kept a little store of medicines and such-like for home use. (Was it not Colet who said, 'If you want wisdom, ask it of God, not of the College of Physicians'?) These consisted of grey powders, friar's balsam, laudanum, senna, arnica to rub on places which seemed out of joint (but they also used the horse embrocations for that), and ointment made from marsh-mallows for sore legs. She even had a recipe for the English cholera, '40 drops oil of peppermint, 80 drops laudanum, $\frac{1}{2}$ pint best brandy. One tablespoonful of the above with an equal quantity of warm water, generally gives relief in ten minutes, but if it does not, repeat the dose.' Incidentally, cholera came to the coast towns as epidemics, brought in by fishermen. There was an outbreak of Asiatic Cholera in Lowestoft in 1848–9.

Both grandparents felt the cold, particularly grandmother. The bed was warmed each night with the old round-faced pan that hung near the hearth, being filled with glowing embers from the fire. How nice it was to creep into such a warmth and snuggle down into the billows of the bed! When grandmother grew older, her gals clubbed together and made a nightdress of yards and yards of white flannel, and they trimmed it with narrow lace. It was ample and full enough to make frost itself sweat, and it was so comfortable and nice to sleep in; but the very dickens to get out of on a cold morning!

But they were not the only couple who felt the cold, and some were not as well off as they, for it must be remembered that too often poverty and cold go hand in hand. These poor old people would warm a brick, wrap it up in flannel and take that to bed with them; or they would use the oven door in the same way, especially after baking. Then when blankets got thin, they would sew sheets of brown paper together, put those in between the old bed clothes; and wonderfully good they were.

Of such were poor old Charlie Chambers and his wife Sophy who lived over by the Yew Tree Corner; they also suffered from the cold. Once Charlie confided in grandmother, 'Oi were so cold, Missus Barham, Oi took my limbs to bed!' Poor old simple-hearted Charlie belonged to that small number who never found pleasure in running down others. When anything of a contentious nature came his way he would remark with an air of great wisdom, 'Well there, some fooks ar'n't all alike!' He was reputed to be so poor that he couldn't afford candles from the shop so he would light his missus to bed by means of a hemlock stalk dipped in brimstone, which he held aloft in the tiny well of the stairway. 'Are you in, gal?' he would enquire as she scrabbled in between the welter of clouts that passed for bed linen. To be answered with, 'Ye . . e . . s, bor, thankee!'

Then, one day towards his end, grandmother met him slowly making his way to the Street. He answered her greetings with, 'Yis, Missus Barham, I'm walking very slow; but there, I'm going fast!'

Baker Free didn't feel the cold as much as Naomi his wife, and he was wont to go off to bed before her. She would not venture between the sheets before taking the chill off them with the old warming-pan. How Baker did hate this business and how scared he was lest she should even touch him with the pan! One night, feeling a bit playsome, and it not being too cold, she took up an empty pan and proceeded to push it about as usual. Presently she gave it that extra push sideways so that it touched Baker's back. Out he flew, shrieking, 'Thare you be, Naomi, you ha' burnt me this time! I told you you would.'

PARENT OF THE BLISSFUL HOUR

As one, awakened from a vision sweet,
Wishes to sleep and dream it o'er again.

◇◇

ALTHOUGH grandmother's home was so old, its interior was really no older than the eighteenth century and, for that matter, no newer. Curiously enough, as one went from one relationship to another in the village, so it was the same. The setting might be different, as for example the Dove House where lived great-aunt Rebecca. This was reached by climbing over a hog-backed stile, walking between orchard trees, and crossing a green sward before you reached the old house. The honeysuckle in those hedges in that quiet retreat away from the road was particularly fragrant. Now this Rebecca was a little better off than Susannah, and if anything, her rusks were better than grandmother's, also she had a settee of crimson repp, and not one of black shiny cloth like her sister-in-law, and she cut her stilton with a silver scoop and not a knife. But just as Dove House was contemporary with Rackford Farm, so its interior was Georgian, of the ample period in furnishing before Victoria came to the throne.

Yet as the furnishing might be of a kind, those old interiors varied from one another structurally. One would have an ecclesiastical-looking niche in the wall (the sort of thing so often used by the old Flemish flower painters as a setting for their exquisite bouquets), and just right to hold a clock; another would have corbelled ledges in the mantel over the fireplace; yet another a canopy over the fireplace, which was the hearth of the room above, jutting down below the ceiling in the room below. In grandmother's case it was a window set in the wall facing the fireplace of her living-room, which looked into her pantry. Once upon a time that had

47

been an outside wall, but extensions being necessary, a lean-to pantry was added; but the window remained. In the pantry amongst the willow-pattern china, ringed mugs and rat-tailed spoons, was an old Dutch clock, so that time, usually so portentous and stately even in a cottage, was also muted, and one had to open the door to see the hour!

There was but one room downstairs, into which the front door opened directly, and out of which another door led to the backhouse, which was in reality a lean-to scullery, yet fairly spacious. All these old rooms seemed to have a wonderful collection of doors, and when it was right cold, as sometimes in January, there was a difficulty in keeping the place warm. This was attempted by several devices, the chief one, being sausage-like objects made of turkey twill and filled with sand, and placed along the bottoms of doors. What they lacked in effectiveness, they made up for in appearance, for red is a protective colour and gives warmth by suggestion.

Grandmother was a bit of a sybarite, liking ease and warmth and bright colours, and like other countrywomen red was her favourite. It cropped up in so many ways: red flannel for petticoats and stays, and to put on grandfather's chest; red garters for rheumatism; a horseshoe on the wall for luck and to keep away witches, covered skin-tight in red; and the same for a brick on the floor to act as a doorstop. Even grandfather's nightcap in winter was of the same comfortable shade, carrying out the injunction given by a certain Dr. Andrew Borde in 1557, 'Let your nyght cap be of scarlet.' But when it came to a question of fitness, it was a colour that accorded ill with his florid complexion. There was more of this shade, for the chief chair in the room, a splendid creation with ample arms and certain lovely curves, was also draped in this same turkey twill, and looked splendid, growing as it were out of the coco-matting. It was grand-

Middleton
Church

The Mill,
Middleton

Carting from the field

Thrashing in the Stowmarket area

father's chair and also a commode. The colour could be seen again in the window which had glistering white blinds:

> And how the crowded cottage sill
> Glows with red geraniums still.

Grandmother's chair was a simple armchair of Regency pattern, with a black shiny seat, a foil to the red. It had low arms and was just right for her to sit and work with her needle to the light given by a couple of composite candles. And, in passing, have you ever seen a case of needles such as grandmother used? If so you would be impressed with their tiny size, and you would wonder how she ever managed to thread them.

In the middle of the wall facing the window was a chest of drawers with brass drop handles. It was a most useful piece, for the drawers held all kinds of things needed in their everyday life. If you looked at it a bit closely you might have noticed that it was in two parts. Undoubtedly in its earlier years it had gone to sea, and unlike so many others of its kind had come home again, to be landed on some English quay, possibly Slaughden, before it found its way into an auction, and into grandfather's kitchen parlour. On top, besides various boxes and the Bible, was the old harnser, standing there unblinkingly amid a sandy pebbly shore, and to one side in a smaller case, a shelduck in similar state. The gun that had shot them stood in the corner.

This room then, with its ample fireplace, one or two silhouettes around the mantel (no relation whatever, but looking nice, some by the great Edouart himself), and a piece or two of lustre commemorating Mr. Wesley, was their home. It was the picture which came into the minds of their children living in sordid suburbia, when they wrote letters home. But, curiously enough, it was not the place to which they wished to return to live. A holiday yes, a fortnight of country fare, and then back to the grime! Times had changed since grandmother was a little girl with no thoughts of leaving her native village. She would have pined away if that had been forced upon her, but with her girls it had been different and those old trains she could hear going over the pile-bridge when the wind lay in that direction had brought it all about.

Grandmother was a good needlewoman; that had been part of her training as well as those other accomplishments of how to brew, bake and put down a pig; and one of her chief pleasures was the making of patchwork quilts. These were composed of octagons, usually of silk, framed in a border of lilac dimity. She loved colours and the feel of expensive materials, which came to her from the same source as the straw bonnet in which she was married. Sometimes Mrs. Doughty would even descend from her carriage, come into the room and watch grandmother at work.

This was indeed a labour of love, and grandmother's *pièce de résistance* measured 99 inches long by 84 inches wide (nearly square you will notice, for use on those old four-posters), and contained 5,930 patches. That took some years to make, and if you multiply the patches by the stitches it would come to a sum far beyond the reckoning of even Mrs. Davey herself. This work was usually done on a paper base, often of old letters, and sometimes when the papers were left in one got a rather curious yet irritating glimpse into a forgotten past. It was rather like this:

Oh my dar
piness. I know
lease your fathe
miserable
n IV.

you say
Kismet again
Go to India. I
hearted
Farew

e my
nnot marr
unworthy
Sacrifice
dieu.

And sometimes the writing was smudged, as though by tears.

Immediately by the fireplace was a narrow little door, and when unsnecked, it disclosed the staircase, an evil, steep winding stairway that clung to the old chimney for support and then burst straight into the parlour chamber above, as the best bedroom was called, without ceremony.

The stairs were composed of brick risers and oak treads some 2 inches thick, scrubbed white and clean. A little hand-rail was to one side, as shining and as smooth as glass, but it was too low and too slanting to be of much use. Going up was not so bad, but coming down was—that is, to come down on one's feet.

The floor boards were of wide chestnut planks, fastened down with hand-made nails, and the floor was carpeted with shred rugs, and polished with beeswax until it shone and was positively dangerous.

Grandmother loved her old bed, which stood four square in the centre of the room close to the well of the staircase, and was so heavy that it was never moved from the day it was erected until both were dead, and it fell under the hammer. It had come to them via an auction, and was of mahogany, with slender fluted pillars at the foot end, and hung with yellow 'stuff' curtains (at least that is what she called them, by which she meant they were not of silk). The bed consisted first of a thick coarse sacking material, laced to the great wooden sides, and on this was a wheat straw mattress or palliasse, made and renewed by grandfather in the barn from thrashings of the harvest. Then came a real down bed, grandmother's pride, made of the finest pickings of goose feathers, result of many Michaelmases.

It was a difficult matter to get into bed, particularly as they got older, so there was a nightstool on grandmother's side with a step or two. This gave her just that lift up to enable her to climb in. Before that, however, she would place a chamber candlestick near at hand, and a box of matches; just in case. (I can see those large matchboxes now, bearing a magnificent trophy of arms that was continental in splendour; and the matches had a smell to match. A most lovely sulphurous aroma that lingered for some minutes after the match had been struck.) Grandfather would wind up his turnip and place it in the embroidered pocket provided for the purpose, that hung at the head of the bed, pinned to the curtains. Then, both having said their prayers, grandmother would place her shoes very carefully, upside down, toes pointing under the bed, to keep herself from having the cramp. Grandfather had taken his precaution before coming up and left his boots in the hearth downstairs, one coming, one going, for the very same purpose! And if grandmother should forget, which she never did, she would have hopped out of bed right quick and put the matter right, otherwise she would not have slept.

Not often were they disturbed, yet sometimes this did happen. It is not nice to be awakened out of sleep, particularly when it is a feather bed that seems to hold you in its arms, but those who have animals in their care are always prone to disturbance, and so was the doctor. His window was often tapped at, and since it was his job he would go, come wind come weather. With grandfather it was different, it was usually a four-footed animal, but sometimes it came about like this. A handful of small pebbles would come rattling against those tiny panes of glass, and out of bed he would scramble:

'What's troublin' you, partner?'

'I'm right sorry, Mister Barham, my wife's time ha' com', an' I ha' gort to go a nidgettin'. Can I hev Scott an' the tumbril? I want to fetch Nuss Fuller an' her box?'

It must have been a rather curious little scene, grandfather sticking out his head, his rubicund face topped by a coquelicot cap, and the suppliant agitated according to the size of his family already. Sometimes grandfather would give his assent with, 'Don't you worry, partner!' At others it would be a grunt, and as he returned to the sheets, a muttered 'That's the tharteenth time, blaarm them!'

On the ground floor of the cottage, in the backhouse (possibly from bake-house, spelt in old wills, 'bakhows'), were two accessories that were of great importance to life. One was in the corner, against the outer wall, the old brick oven, and the other was next to it, the copper. Without these two life would have been poor indeed.

The brick oven came to life on a Friday when faggots were brought in from the wood store just outside, and were fed into the smooth, clean, almost shining little tunnel of bricks and stones that was the oven. It had no chimney and no grating. This kilnware, as it was called, was fired, the oven door, shaped like a flat shield, was closed, and the fire allowed to burn itself out. When this was done, the door, which was loose and not hinged, was removed and the ashes were either raked out or brushed to one side. Then into the red-hot chamber went the baking for the week, ending up with the batch of bread, and the weekly joint, if they had one. The smell when this delectable food was brought out on the end of the peel (a long-handled implement with an iron spoon, one in use and the other at the blacksmith's being laid) had to be experienced to be believed. As the loaves cooled off, standing on the table, so the small home was filled with an incense that was only equalled by the taste.

One can picture grandmother, her face framed by her cap, usually pale, but now flushed by the heat of the oven, working vigorously away with her peel, stepping over the bits of kindling on the floor. Brushing away some loose ash here, and almost overcome with the steam as the table became loaded, and the oven filled and emptied by turns. And the children getting in the way, which was something they did not do on washdays.

One of grandmother's specialities was her rusks. These, made from the dough, baked crisp and buttered, were a standby for all occasions. To be munched with a cup of tea, or if you had no teeth, to be crumbled in the cup; or eaten with a glass of home-made wine. If made according to the old recipe, then something to be remembered and longed after. Here then is her recipe: 'To two pounds of dough add 2 ozs. lard, 2 ozs. butter and 2 eggs. These to be well worked with the hands, moistened with milk, sprinkled with flour and kept for a time. Break down the mixture again and stiffen up.'

In the corner beside the peel, sometimes crossed as it were in saltire, was the fork. This was for putting the faggots into the oven; and hanging on the door leading into the kitchen parlour was a goose wing for sweeping clear the mouth of the oven.

Which brings us to the copper, which *was* of copper, and not of zinc as in later days. It was scoured clean with red brick dust from rotten bricks. It shone, like every other bit of metal then in daily use and was used for brewing two or three times a year, washing once a month, and for cooking puddings at Harvest and Christmas. It had a capacious furnace that was fed by all kinds of odds and ends which if allowed to survive would have become museum pieces. It had an intricate chimney that could only be kept clear by a charge of gunpowder.

A reminder of washday was a pair of wooden legs that hung by the wall. These were for stretching grandmother's stockings lest they shrank whilst they dried. Wood ash was taken from the oven and made into a lye for the washing, and a gentle abrasive in the cleaning of wood surfaces until they glistened.

Another piece in that backhouse worthy of mention was the flour boulter. This was in the shape of a chest of drawers, painted grey, apparently consisting of three drawers, but in reality there was only one, the bottom drawer into which the flour fell. You lifted the lid, poured in a sack of flour on to an inclined plane which led to a revolving brush, turned the handle, and out came the middlings by a chute at the side. It was a money saver, and anything that did that was welcome in a house of so few shillings a week. When half a comb of flour a week was sent to the mill for grinding, and the meal refined in this box, it saved as much as a shilling and four pounds of flour—a considerable amount.

And there on a handy hook, ready, was grandfather's horn lantern, which was a close link with the Middle Ages. How often in those old church accounts figures the item of 'leaves for the lanthorn'? It was of real necessity in those days, wanted in an emergency to spill a little light and show the way to an animal in distress. (I think grandfather was a bit of a vet, because hanging in the backhouse, when I was a tiny visitor there, was his fleam stick, used for bleeding cattle. It was full of dents.)

How pleasant that old lantern looked, with its rusty, crinkled outline, as though it would fall to pieces at any time! It had grimy leaves of horn, a tiny hinged door that snecked into a worn upright, and a conical top full of jagged little slits and a series of domed oval louvres. When the tallow candle was lit these airlets seemed to give out more light than the horn, as also they gave out a fine smell when the candle was blown out and the lantern returned to its hook. Since its ancestry was uncertain (like some of the village children) it was probable that it had lit a few smuggling episodes on the nearby marshes.

One of grandmother's axioms was, 'As we brew so we must bake,' and considering the yeast from the former went into the latter and determined what sort of bread came out of the oven, there was a philosophy of life even in her backhouse. And she didn't want anyone 'a pampling' over her floor after she had cleaned up!

It must also be remembered that it was at her backhouse door that grandmother received her callers, since no one in the country used the front door for such purposes, that being reserved for funerals. It is the case today at many a country cottage, even those inhabited by so-called gentry. The adults would, more often than not, address her as 'Missus Barham,' but the children preferred just plain Susannah, and no offence meant or taken.

The usual approach was, 'How do you fare this marnin', ma'am?' To which the reply would be, whatever the season or the indication on the health chart, 'Oh, moderate, thankee!' Sometimes she would declare she felt like a 'toad under a harrer,' but she seldom looked like it. Some would only *pake* their heads over the half-hatch door, but the more intimate would cross the threshold and sit down on one of the two seggen-bottomed turned ash chairs that had been painted green at some time since they were first made in the reign of Queen Anne.

One of her callers who came often, especially in late years when her gals were away 'in sarvice,' or married, was Reuben Noy the postman. He was always glad when he had 'suffen' for the house, even if it was only a begging letter, because he knew he would find a little refreshment. After all, he had to walk eighteen miles a day, and half that on Sundays, for 9s. 6d. a week, and he was glad of a rest. Besides he was often useful in keeping grandmother informed about the health of outlying villagers, such as Mariah Newstead's husband, John, who lived up by Title.

'How is cousin John?' she would ask.

'Oh, he's butter!' would come the soft genial reply of Reuben, who had an open face that matched the pleasant sound of his name. 'But Bailey won't let him get up. And do you know, Missus Barham, he will keep a gettin' out o' bed!'

'I don't like the sound of that too much,' grandmother would reflect, as she busied herself buttering a rusk and pouring out a mug of small beer.

'No, but John ha' allus been a bit headstrong. Mariah say

she'll manage him, so she did, she fenced his bed with fuz bushes, an' that have settled him for the time being.'

It was a long long day since the road past that cottage of grandmother's was used by the peddars, but even in her day their descendants came to her backhouse door, and they were welcome although her pennies were few. After all, peddars were before shops, and country people even in our advanced times like to do their business on their own door-step. Not everyone cares to go into a shop, evidently some ancient subconscious fear or antipathy still lurking in their bucolic upbringings. The travelling salesman finds some of his best and most reliable customers at cottage back doors. And they will take what he cares to bring, not being over-fastidious. So then it was not surprising to find the haberdasher woman, Mary Mullinger, amongst grandmother's callers.

She came almost apologetically, crab-like, with a hamper on her arm covered by a slippery black waterproof cloth. If the outside was black and almost forbidding the inside was quite different, for it was lined with coloured sprigged material that seemed to set off the dainties within. There were frilled caps, coloured kerchief, buttons and thread, hooks and eyes (these of recent innovation as the old seam-stresses preferred tiny buttons and button-holes), needles and pins, darning wool and cottons in hanks, many of them done up in penn'orths and ha'p'orths. All these were offered with the restrained gentility of old-world manners.

Naturally enough Eliza and Rebecca found a good deal to discuss in Mary Mullinger. Eliza was sure she lived in a little red sitting-room, somewhere Kelsale way, where an enormous kettle was always boiling on the hob. 'I'd like to go and have a peep, wouldn't you, Becca?'

Rebecca said if it meant going past the Round House (reputed to be haunted), then she wasn't anxious. 'Besides,' she continued, 'they say she keep silkworms, and stays in bed to hatch out the eggs by the heat of her body!'

'Oh, well there,' replied Eliza, 'like old Jessie Pipe at Theberton, when she was laid up. She kinder sat on thirteen eggs, and brought them off! Still, I reckon Mary will be always a sewin', like a tailor at Easter Eve!'

And sometimes these girls managed a copper or two for their bottom drawer, which was a complimentary phrase, since they hadn't got a drawer a-piece in their tiny room. (Incidentally, American girls have adapted the phrase to a Hope Chest.)

Yet another caller was Aaron Selfe from Westleton, who peddled fish in a great ped or hamper, which he carried on his head; as though he and the basket had entered life together. He would walk miles to any outlandish place if he thought they could do with his fish. When he got on in years, his boys thought they would get him a donkey to help the wear and tear on his neck. But with the donkey came a great affection and concern into Aaron's heart concerning the animal. He would take it to the inn and give it a pint of beer, which the donkey thoroughly enjoyed, holding back its head and swallowing every drop. Then, if Aaron thought the way too rough, or the load too heavy, he would stick the basket on his head as before and trudge beside his friend, keeping it company. In fact, if necessary he would have carried the donkey as well!

THE SHELTER'D COT, THE CULTIVATED FARM

I'll lay me down on the green sward,
Mid yellowcups and speedwell blue,
And pay the world no more regard,
But be to Nature leal and true.

GRANDFATHER'S village was there in the time of the Domesday Survey, low lying in the marshes, and shards of Romano-British pottery have been found. There are really two main groupings of the 'housen,' the one about the Green by the church, known as the Street, and the other on higher ground a mile away known as the Moor. This latter is a much larger green, and in grandfather's time was noted for the large flocks of geese maintained there by the surrounding cottagers. But there is only one inn in the parish, thatched like the church, and hidden in a corner of the Street. The inn-keeper was also a farmer. A similar inn, also called 'The Bell,' was painted by Morland.

The windmill, that other village feature which twizzled so merrily in grandfather's day, towered above the cottages on a slight rise in the scene, seeming to rival the church as a distinguishing feature. Its round house still remains. Inside, covered with mealy dust, was an old notice board bearing black Roman letters on a white background. It said:

The Rules of This Mill

	s.	d.
For Grinding Wheat per Bushel of 8 Gallons	o	8
For do. Beans, Pease, Barley, etc.	o	7
Bolting per Bushel	o	2

To this mill the small one-horsed farmer carried his corn in sacks slung across his horse's back, as had been the custom from time immemorial.

A story was current about this mill, concerning a village lad named John Doy, who was powerfully built and of exceptional strength in his wrists. He wagered that he could hold on to one of the sails and be carried round for one sweep. This happened at the end of the Napoleonic Wars, and evidently provided a village celebration of a novel kind. Anyway, he won his bet, and the villagers must have looked on open mouthed and ox-eyed with wonder.

Grandfather could remember the new rectory being built, but it has mellowed now into a pleasant, square little country house. In its paddock grew the largest single snowdrops that were ever seen. Grandmother knew, since she was allowed a bunch to sweeten her room, gathered in the sharp damp of early morning. Before the door, on the lawn, grew a beautiful magnolia, planted by Mr. White himself, brought home from one of his travels. Each year in early spring it bursts into flowers that shine in the sunlight and burn softly in the rain. Sad to relate, it is beginning to feel its age, and shows signs of a decline. Although new in that time-corroded scene yet that rectory was reputed to be haunted; not by some learned doctor—'as pale as the candle he studied by'—but by a backhouse boy. It was said he would open the doors leading from the kitchen quarters to the living apartments, despite weights being placed to keep them shut, and work away at a pump in the midst of the stone-flagged kitchen; always about midnight. Could it have been that he had enjoyed living there so much that he had decided to remain in spite of churchyard ceremonies? The comment of the villagers was, at least those who knew, 'All them heapin' pails o' water wasted: that whooly seem a shame!' The old rectory is still there, a building that has been refurbished, but the slope of the roof tells that it dates with the rest of the village and from the time when the rector farmed his glebe. Again rumours had been at work, and it was said that one of that old cloth had kept a 'lovely' there; but folks will talk. The tithe-barn, an imposing feature then, but which slowly mouldered away in grandfather's time stood between the rectory and the inn, facing Duffers' meadows.

Farms and farmsteads were dotted about the parish. There was the Dove House Farm, Hawthorn Farm, Packway Farm, Hill Farm, Trust Farm, Garden House Farm, with Rackford Farm on the east side; while Moor Farm, Fen Street Farm, Causeway Farm, Fir Tree Farm and Water Mill Farm were to the west. Then, at the extremity of the sister parish came Fordley Hall which had long since become a farmhouse, together with its own Home Farm. It is divided from the by-road by a paddock that held one or two stag-headed oaks, and its old mullioned windows glinted in the setting sun and were sombre in the shade. Tales enough to fill an evening before a cheerful fire were told of this ancient house, since it was certainly haunted. For example, shadows were apt to precede one when walking along its passages, or on entering some of the rooms. Doors also opened and closed, and there was the sound of footsteps when no human person moved. Upstairs, near the clock-turret (one of those clocks with no face but which struck the hours), in the corner was a red stain in the floor that could not be removed, scrub and scour as one might. It would always come through red again, sure sign of some ancient evil deed, so they said. In the large stone-flagged floor of the outer kitchen was a well, so deep that it took a stone two whole minutes to reach the water with a dull, hollow, muffled plump! Nearby was a huge cheese-press that looked like a rack out of Foxe's *Book of Martyrs*, and everywhere smelt dank and damp like a dungeon.

But that was not all, for in the stackyard was an immense stone, evidently one of those glacial sandstone boulders associated with witches, and sometimes found isolated in a field. Under this, so folks said, lay a treasure trove. As it was somewhat in the way, the farmer had a team of horses attached to a trace fastened to a girdle running round the stone; but those horses were powerless even to move it, although being Punches they went down on their knees to it. It was vouched for as a meeting-place for a coven of witches by Fred Vincent himself, who had seen them. And as all the world knows there is no pub near it, for it is about midway between Middleton 'Bell' and Kelsale 'Eight Bells.' However, children came to this stone with a supply of pins, which they would stick into the natural holes, run round it several times as fast as they could scamper, then put their ears to it, listening in the hope, rather than the dread, of hearing the Devil speak!

Apart from the farmhouses and the rectory, there was not a house of any distinction in the village, so there are no hatchments in the church, but there were and are one or two little villas occupied by retired couples, elderly spinsters or widows. One of these, known as Kensington Villa, along by the Causeway, housed as curious a couple as could be found in any village; they lived a sort of weather-chart existence. Old man James had a strong masculine pride, while Sukey his wife was rather simple. Every now and again John James imagined himself to be affronted by her and would tell her sharply—'Sukey! Walk out!' The simple, innocent little woman would then take up a stand just outside the parlour door, in meek obedience. After a few moments of such penance John would relent, and in milder accents announce—'Sukey! Walk in! My conscience accuses me!'

The one and only shop was kept by an enterprising man with a huge beard, and they used to say in their rude country fashion that when he visited the barber, the latter would remark, 'Evenin', Mister Broom, the beard 'll pay for the shavin'!' and then laugh. He had a numerous family, was related to grandfather in some involved sort of way, and had two somewhat worthless sons—Alma, obviously named after topical events, and Azor, source unknown. However, neither Alma nor Azor were of any use to their father and his business, and both died at an early age of too many visits to the 'Bell.' It was said of Broom senior, that he suffered from *psoriasis palmarum*, or grocer's itch, but then everyone suffered from something of the kind, particularly the lawyers. And in those days there were fleas and even bugs in the best houses, the former being very apparent at barley sowing and barley mowing.

The shop (evidently referred to in the Overseers' Accounts for 1791—'Laid out for her at Lambert's shop, £1.19.0') was of that nice old village type, now almost extinct, consisting of two bow windows composed of small panes of glass, with a door between them. Over the door was a neat little sign of local writing, black on white. It said:

Joseph Broom
Licensed Dealer
In Tea, Tobacco
& Snuff.

The shop floor was a study in composition and adhesion, since it consisted of the craziest of paving. Large flat stones, bricks and odd shaped wide planks of wood from the saw pit, all set in to be as level as such an assortment could be.

The shop was crammed from floor to ceiling with all kinds of things that country folk could possibly want or could be cozened into parting with their money for, and it had its own peculiar spicy smell that was part of it. Even the children could find something here, if they were lucky enough to have a penny to spend, but I doubt if they could have bought a flat-iron for a farthing, or even a grid-iron, a dish, and two plates for the same amount, as did Mrs. Ewing Ritchie's dear little girls. However, Broom had certain eye-catcher bottles of sweets made of sugar mixed with lard, and biscuits stamped *Albert's Fancy* and *Victoria Cakes*, the latter bearing a royal crown; and nearer Christmas a few Dutch dolls, all wooden and ready for small fingers to dress and then cherish for the rest of their lives.

Along one side, behind the counter, was a series of little square-faced drawers, one on the right labelled 'wafers.' There was a sale for these up to the time of the arrival of envelopes; and then their day was done. Above the drawers was a row of tin canisters in green and gold, numbered 1 to 12. These contained tea, which Broom blended according to village tastes, or what he thought was their taste, each blend having a dash of the green to give it the right tang.

In the corner of the wall facing the door was a little store-room devoted to pork butchery. It was a miniature shop in itself, with an ancient block, chopper, knives, and all sorts and kinds of hooks, 'S,' pluck, chine and gambals. Curiously enough, in later years, Broom's eldest daughter, Rhoda (nice name, and a nice clean petite woman was Rhoda), married a Barham, Joseph like her father, and he became the parish pig killer, going from place to place with his appliances in a frail basket (I now possess them as part of my museum). They consisted of buckers, knives, scuds for scraping made from an old scythe blade; and a hook to remove toe nails. His fee was one shilling per pig, and certain appurtenances.

Broom also sold flour, which he kept in a huge wooden hutch and ladled it out with a nice smooth shiny wooden scoop. This was weighed up on beam scales suspended over the counter. If you wanted less than a stone of flour at a time you went to Broom, but if more then to the mill. Paper in those days was scarce, so customers had to provide their own wrappings, which when it came to flour was a pillow-case.

Cheeses were kept separately. First they had to be skinned, then cut in half and quarters by a curiously shaped knife like a battle-axe, as used in 1066.

The third wall of the shop, that is the one on the right as you entered, was devoted to the drapery and napery which

A giant has fallen. For barking the trunks the man on the right is holding a body iron, while the two men in the branches are using wrong irons for the wrongs or branches of trees

Beating the bounds at Hasketon or Burgh, c.1888

The Middleton band

Bradfield St. Clare, about 1880

Broom also sold. Calico in large quantities since it was used for underclothing, village girls' trousseaux, and instead of paper, as even butter was wrapped up in napkins made of calico. Then there were printed cottons in which lilac seemed to predominate with puce and magenta, the inevitable turkey twill and red flannel.

There were also coloured handkerchiefs, of which Broom was very proud. In his young days they had grown into positive news-sheets in an attempt to escape the Newspaper Tax. They were even used for educational purposes acting as spelling primers, and were printed in much the same way as the battledores that had succeeded the horn books.

Broom sold everything and could look his customers in the face, for if any monkeying about with the commodities had been attempted it was before he had the goods. 'If your "strong black" tea tastes of ink, examine it with a magnet, to see if it contains iron, added to cheat you in weight.' And since you had no magnet you had to put up with it and could merely grumble that a spoonful didn't go so far as it did when dear Aunt Sophy was alive. But be sure it wasn't Broom's fault. However, he was not above pandering to vanities and whimsies although he was a pronounced radical and a chapel-goer. For instance he kept a whole cask of hair-oil, for the use and aggrandisement of rustic youth on the Sabbath. He found a sale for this on a Saturday night, and the result was exhibited in the church the next day, in a row of sleek glossy heads smelling strangely. Those, of course, who could not afford this resorted to lard or mutton fat.

Then he sold crockery and ornaments, pretty little bits from Staffordshire which, down the years, either got broken or became great treasures. Wall-papers of those nice little flowered stripes that made a little room appear larger. These, by the way, were applied one on top the other until as many as thirty or forty thicknesses were on those old walls, and you could drive a nail into them to hold up a 'gay' (picture). Vinegar from the cask, although there was a lot of sour beer about, as sour as wadges (? verjuice). Folk would send their children for 'a penn'orth o' winegar, if you plaize!' to be greeted with one of Broom's little jokes. 'Well, there, partner, tell yare mother my winegar ha' all gone sour!' However, under the casks were his bright shining measures ranging from a gill to a pint, and stamped with the insignia of the local Weights and Measures Authority, which was at Yoxford, some going back to the Georges, but others with a new 'V.R.'

The currants took a deal of cleaning. First they were dug out from the tightly packed box by an ancient two-pronged fork (again in my museum), and then they were rubbed round and round in a sieve until the fingers almost bled. Sugar, however, had to be broken off the cone by the breaker that was fixed on the end of the counter, whereas sugar of the baser sort, 'moist brown,' was again liable to deceit and had to be dug out of a bin and weighed up into pounds as required. It was said of this that it contained dirt, sand and mites, but as many other things of daily consumption held even more of these adulterations it didn't seem to matter much. However, 'if dissolved in warm water, the heavy dirt falls to the bottom and the mites float on the surface, affording an interesting object for the microscope.' Well, who in that village had a microscope, and who cared? Then he sold lots of treacle, doled out into basins by a wooden spoon, because this was the children's fare smeared over their bread, often by a brush. But if either Alma or Azor, slightly dizzied by beer, left the tap a-jar at night when Broom slept, then the treacle would 'sue' out and make a molasses flood. But as Broom was a large and religious grocer it was wonderful how he could skate round the general vocabulary of naughty words and vent his feelings without using one of the accepted variety.

Broom was nothing if not enterprising, so to increase his business he not only:

> Made Alphabets of ginger-bread
> That folks might swallow what they read,

which he did to deck his stall erected on the Green on Whit Monday, but he travelled 'up parish and down parish,' and outside its boundaries, calling on those who found it difficult to call on him. They were pleased to see him at Theberton where their own shopkeeper had a temper as sour as his own vinegar. For this purpose Broom had a little covered cart, drawn by a pair of mongrel dogs, Ben and Dan, as cunning as ever a pair could be. They not only worked well in harness, but worked together in ratting like players in a football field. The roof of that little cart existed for many years after Broom's death, rotting away under the currant bushes behind the shop, and as traction by dogs ceased in 1854 it was fairly old when I saw it.

There was often a bit of banter in this backdoor business.

'You're givin' extra good measure this mornin', Mr. Broom!'

'Ah, well, ma'am, my poor old father used to say—"Hape it up bor! Hape it up! Good weight and measure is heavenly treasure!" '

On the other hand he could be a bit tight for he had been known to cut a raisin in half to achieve the just balance, screwing up his mouth as he did so.

Broom also grew into the first Postmaster, anticipating that office by providing a box on his counter into which those customers who could write could drop their letters. They were then handed to the postman who came into the village on horseback, sounding a horn to announce his arrival. In due time Broom was installed as Middleton's first Postmaster, and the office remained in his family for ninety-nine years. In time, therefore, there appeared a bill hanging up near his sloping desk with the spindle-rail top. It stated:

> To all Postmasters and Sub-Postmasters,
> General Post Office,
> 25 April, 1840.

It has been decided that Postage Stamps are to be brought into use forthwith, and as it will be necessary that every such Stamp should be cancelled at the Post Office or Sub Post Office where the letter bearing the same may be posted, I herewith forward for your use, an Obliterating Stamp, with which you will efface the Postage Stamp upon every letter despatched from your office. Red Composition must be used for the purpose, and I annex directions for making it, with an Impression of the Stamp.

As the stamps will come into operation by the 9th of May, I must desire that you will not fail to provide yourself with the necessary supply of Red Composition by that time.

Directions for Preparing the Red Stamping Composition.

1 lb. Printer's Red Ink.

1 pt. Linseed Oil.

Half a pint of the droppings of Sweet Oil.

To be well mixed.

> By Command
> W. L. MABERLEY, *Secretary*.

One wonders how many of the famous Penny Black Broom sold, with the instructions printed on the strip below the block—'Address towards the Right-Hand Side of the Letter. In Wetting the Back be careful not to Remove the Cement.' A strip of seven unused Penny Blacks recently sold for £400 in Bond Street.

Not much excitement came to the village, save an occasional fire. Owing to the nature and shape of the coastline and its proximity to the sea, it seemed removed from the rest of the world. The main turnpike, which ran from London to Yarmouth, was some three miles westward, and eastwards there were but lonely marshes that ran down to the sea. Therefore, the only contact with the rest of the world was westward, or by foreign influences imported into it. One of these, not unwelcome, was the gipsies. They came, no one knew whence, and went, no one knew whither, setting up their umbrella-tented encampment on the Moor.

Shy traffickers, the dark Iberians came.

They were the real thing, the Picketts, Lees or Smiths, and were not merely caravan dwellers with whining, supplicating voice, but dark-eyed, dark-haired men, the finest appraisers of horse flesh; and women who had the future of weal or woe in their hands. They spoke Romany, at least when negotiating deals in horses, and that added to the air of mystery which surrounded them. They appealed to the country heart, since they knew the stars, the future, and more effective cures than Bailey with all his doctor's learning. Then they travelled and were therefore so different from those who lived and died in one place.

Their wagons were brightly coloured and above the gently curved roof, the stove-pipe chimney smoked. There were twisted gold pillars and curtains at the little windows and door. One gipsy, Rodney Smith, had a particularly fine caravan, with the usual little platform at the back before a half-hatch door. But it also had a spindle-faced gallery that ran from the platform along each side for the matter of some three feet. These formed two little pens for his travelling farmyard of geese and chickens. They hopped out sprightly enough when the caravan rested on the Moor and delighted in the fine lush grass.

Sometimes the gipsies gave a ball, lighting bonfires at the

three corners of the Moor and hanging lamps on their vans. The women wore black dresses and decked themselves out with red and blue ribbons while the men dressed themselves in the clothes they wore when they went to a big market or Horse Fair. (One of the latter was held at Colfer [Cold Fair] Green, Knodishall, and descendants of the gipsies have settled there.) Their women could dance, tirelessly and with fine abandon. On one such occasion, Colonel White (Mr. White's brother) went to watch, *incognito*, of course, and remarked that it was much like an Indian *natch*. As for grandfather, he preferred to keep out of their way, for he had a wholesome respect for their remarkable knowledge even of others' quite private affairs.

Fairs were the chief source of village excitement, but they were outside, and one had to walk to them, which most people were glad to do. There had been two at Dunwich, relics of its former greatness. St. James's Fair, held on the 5th, 6th and 7th of November. Then another and famous Fair which still exists, at Southwold on Trinity Monday. There was another at Framlingham—in fact Middleton was ringed with them, but they were all a long way off. That was no deterrent, since folk were used to footing it, and as many as could jogged off to enjoy the fun, the best time being on the eve to watch the raggle-taggle procession coming in. There were the usual raucous attractions and a few striking contrasts, such as a Living Skeleton, a man twenty-four years of age who weighed only 3 stone, and Daniel Lambert of Leicester who weighed 52 stone 11 pounds, and had to have a special chair made to sit on. What a pity, thought some of those old countrymen, he wasn't born a hog! There might even be Betsy Boffin, who the advertisement announced, was 'born without Arms, Hands and Legs. She is comely of appearance, twenty-five years of age and is only 37 inches high, by astonishing means she has invented and practised in attaining the use of the needle, scissors, pen, pencil . . . she can cut out and make any part of her own clothes, sews, writes well, draws landscapes, paints miniatures and many other more wonderful things, all of which she performs principally with Her Mouth.'

But perhaps the best turn was the Dancing Egyptian, dressed in a flame-coloured silk gown, tight fitting, and confined over the hips by a large shawl. An enormous pair of chintz drawers completed her costume. Her dark hair was braided (some said it was smeared with castor oil), and her chin and lips were tattooed with blue spots, while her eyelids were painted black and her hands and feet were yellow. Surpassing all, however, was an enormous gold ring, like a bangle, hanging from her nose over her mouth. She danced to a tambourine and a kettle drum, and as she came to the last dying fall there was an audible expression of admiration in half-suppressed sighs heard passing round the tent. But one must not forget the old saying—'Sugar candy comes from Egypt.'

There were others, the Fortune Tellers, and they did a brisk business, since no trade flourishes better at fairs than superstition. Some of the old women were heard to say it was not worth their while wasting any money there, since their own fortunes were fixed. It was a case of luck and misfortune every morning as far as they were concerned, but now and then some of the younger married women ventured behind the curtain, when they thought no one was looking. One thing was very evident, they didn't go to seek a charm to make themselves fruitful, quite the contrary, it was rather something that would check the increase, or prevent them having any more girls. Young girls, on the other hand, sought advice to make their own particular fancy fall in love with them, and so cure their hot hearts.

Once, however, excitement came to the village, in the shape of a hairy man with a mangy bear on the end of a chain. He was spotted first by the Parish Clerk's wife who rushed out holding the corner of her apron in her hand, ready to put it over her head if need be, and almost at once others followed, including Broom and his two sons Alma and Azor. The poor old bear stood on its hind legs and danced, while the grimy owner chanted what sounded like—'Hoddy-don-don-dey! Alle do ni dah-Farle me-Farle-me-Farle me-Alle do ni dah!' This, the spectators took to be a foreign language, or English as spoken in London. He then threw his staff to the bear who caught it in his arms. Then to everyone's amazement the dirty rascal, as the coppers were so few, asked them in English (not their English, but they understood), if they had got any bread for the bear. Of course they hadn't got any bread, for they only baked enough to last a week. However, that trollop Naomi Lumpkins ran into her one-roomed hovel down by the 'Bell' and brought out a whole loaf that had gone sad, and with great temerity *hulled* it towards Bruin, who caught it wonderfully clever like, and with even greater dexterity than the staff, and having got it, knew what to do with it. Some of the little crowd 'whooly' laughed, while others fair shuddered and deplored such a waste of good 'wittals.'

That was not all, for the next thing they heard was that the man had asked Josiah Mayhew if he could sleep in his outhouse for the night with the bear. Curiously enough, he had hit on the right man, a man too soft hearted to say No, so the whole village was put on tenterhooks until the morning lest the bear should break loose, and find its way into their cottages, or steal their honey. Mrs. Mayhew barricaded her stairs besides setting gin traps at both front and back doors. (She couldn't open her front door in any case.) And poor old Josiah never heard the last of it for a month. 'I reckon he have got more fleas on him than there are feathers in our bed, an' as for that warmint I kind of reckon his hide be that thick they can't get their teeth through nohow. Fancy him a sleeping with his old bear, and in our nice clean shod (it wasn't all that clean), that don't fare to me to be Christian. But there, perhaps, that'll eat him afore the mornin', like that bear did in the Bible.'

'Oh,' replied Josiah softly, hoping to turn away wrath, 'and wat'll we do with the old bear if it do?'

'P'raps then,' she continued, 'the squire 'll come an' shoot him. Then you can skin un an' make his fur into a rug for the parlour.'

The visit of the bear was the subject of conversation in the village for weeks following; the first question being as to where it had come from? Simple old Charlie Chambers said he thought he came from Aldeburgh. 'Oh, ah, yes,' said the others, 'that's all right enough, but where did he come from before he got to Aldeburgh? That's what we want to know.' And since they were not on conversation terms with the squire, his sons, or even the parson, all of whom they felt would have known, they had to take counsel with the village oracle, the now poor and weatherbeaten ex-cavalryman, Charlie Godward.

'Yes,' he said, 'I think I know where he come from, for I have bin there in my time. That's a place called Circassia, and I don't advise any of you together to go, not even if you get the chance.'

'No,' they said, 'that sound a rum old place, is that fudder than London?'

'Yis, yis,' continued Charlie, 'that's over the water, bor. The men are all hairy, and their eyes fare flash, and when they row in their funny little old boats they sing: *Arira-ri-ra* to every stroke. My heart, that sound good! Their wimmen are whooly beautiful too, regular angels, but they don't wear skirts like ours do, they wear coloured silk drawers instead.'

'Do they though,' ejaculated Pepper, 'that's a rum un!'

'Yes,' went on Charlie, 'and do you know you can buy one of them gals for a hoss-load of stuff—if so be as you've got it.'

73

'Bless my heart,' said Pepper, 'why, I got my old missus for nothing,' at which some laughed. 'But there, that remind me o' Frannigan (Framlingham) Fair, where I've been told you can buy a wife for sixpence. They sound to me like a lot of old diddeycoys.'

'Yes,' concluded Charlie, 'p'raps you're right, partner, p'raps you're right!'

PASTORAL SYMPHONY

Lord, 'tis Thy plenty-dropping hand
That soiles my land;
And giv'st me for my bushell sowne,
Twice ten for one.

◇◇

GRANDFATHER'S name belonged to his village by inheritance. There were Barhams everywhere, up at Title, down at the Fen Street, and on the Moor. There was one at the Dove House, another at Fordley Hall, and yet another at the Garden House. Generally speaking they all got on together very well, although sundry little differences sometimes arose through feminine in-laws, but there was a mutual respect since they bore the same name. Of course they were different from one another, a difference, for instance, very marked as in the case of grandfather and his own brother. The former was choleric, effusive, demonstrative, allowing his feelings their full play, while his brother was exactly opposite, taciturn, reflective, giving to the world the air of a philosopher, which he was not. And whereas the one was deeply religious and gave his time and energies to the chapel, the other was political from a Nonconformist angle.

Since grandfather lived in a patriarchal age, and looked the part, with his blue eyes (so very blue and which could see so far, almost into the next world), and scraggly beard that ran along the outline of his cheek-bone, he was steeped in the Bible, and its companion book, Bunyan's *Pilgrim's Progress*. He could read, and saw to it that his children were taught at the local Dame's school at a penny a week each, supplemented by tuition in the Sunday-school. Unconsciously he fulfilled the sentiments expressed by Erasmus that '. . . the husbandman should sing them [the Psalms] as he holds the handles of his plough; the weaver repeat

75

them as he plies his shuttles; and the weary traveller
refresh himself under some shady tree by these goodly
narratives.'

Grandfather was particularly fond of the forty-second
chapter of Genesis, which says: 'Now when Jacob saw there
was corn in Egypt, Jacob said unto his sons, Why do ye
look one upon another? And he said, Behold, I have heard
that there is corn in Egypt: get you down thither and buy for
us from thence; that we may live, and not die. And Joseph's
ten brethren went down to buy corn in Egypt.' Since grandfather could vividly recall the Hungry 'Forties, and other
periods of dark depression, when turnips were stolen from
the fields because of the scarceness and high cost of
bread, he revelled in these passages and entered into
their rustic import, pondering in his mind what kind of
wheat it was the Egyptians grew, and if by chance it was
Talavera. Besides, for him Egypt was somewhere in the
'sheres' (shires).

In more pastoral mood he loved the sixty-fifth Psalm:
'The river of God is full of water: thou preparest their corn,
for so thou providest for the earth. Thou waterest her furrows,
thou sendest rain into the little valleys thereof: thou makest
it soft with the drops of rain, and blessest the increase of it.
. . . The folds shall be full of sheep: the valleys also shall
stand so thick with corn, that they shall laugh and sing.'
He thought that must have been like the Ten Acre or
Winding Field, which ran down to Rackford Run over by
Fordley.

Another of his favourites was the passage in the New
Testament dealing with the Walk to Emmaus. That piece of
road was always associated in his mind with the road across the
Moor running from the Toll Gate to Yoxford; or reversing the
direction, coming along the Turnpike towards the gable-end
of the Moor Farm. It is a stretch of road uncommonly like
that portrayed by Hobbema, with a line of tall elms on either

side and there, in the distance, lying in a fold of his green fields was his church, its spire surmounted by a golden cockerel, standing up distantly in a mediaeval landscape. Just as the Italian Renaissance painters had set the Crucifixion in a background of their own hills, so grandfather gave his Bible a Suffolk setting. 'Did not our hearts burn within us?' Yes, indeed, for his heart was so often hot! (It might be mentioned in passing that Prize Fights used to be held in some of the hollows of the Moor in his day, to be followed later by open-air baptisms in the same spots, when the hollows were filled with water.)

As for the *Pilgrim's Progress*, since it was written in the vocabulary of the common people with long passages containing only words of one syllable, it was well within his scope. Moreover, he could give it a local flavour, and place events and characters amid his own familiar fields. 'Do you see yonder Wicket Gate? Do you see yonder shining light?' How that recalled to him finding his way across unknown paths in a failing light, and not being too sure that some headless black dog, or old Shock himself, would not brush by him! If Bunyan had only used 'hinward' instead of yonder, that would have been pure Suffolk. Then, of course, he knew so well the feeling that had prompted: 'He went like one that was all the while treading on forbidden ground.' Shades of the few occasions when his pockets were lined with partridges' eggs, or one or two rabbits.

Again, grandfather was quite sure that 'Doubting Castle' was Framlingham, and Giant Despair none other than one of the Bigods; while the cave in which dwelt Pope and Pagan must have been at Leiston Abbey, in that reputed underground passage. And as for Vanity Fair? Well, that was Southwold on Trinity Monday, where they gambled for buttons rather than not gamble at all.

Then there was that little incident with the lions barring

the entrance to the Palace, where people walked on the roof. He rather liked that and thought it picturesque. In his mind he could identify that with Theberton House, for rumour had it that somewhere amongst the chimney stacks on the roof of that old stuccoed mansion was a lily pond, and one would only have such a thing in a place so folks could walk about and admire it. But he 'whooly' liked the man who said: 'Set down my name, Sir!'

Of course he knew Talkative of Prating Row; but then who didn't? Also the Waterman, '. . . looking one way and rowing another.' He must have been a turnpike sailor, for you couldn't do that at sea. And, 'so I saw in my dream, that they went on apace before, and Ignorance he came hobbling after.' He could relish that too; but then he never could suffer fools gladly, and was wont to give vent to his wrath in such little aphorisms as:

Calves' heads are best hot
And fools' mouths are best shut.

Then there was the bit which came nearer home, about 'the sow that was washed, returns to her wallowing in the mire.' Who, you might ask, would be so senseless as to wash a rootling sow? Well, there was a farmer in the village who did that sort of thing, Jethro Winter at the Moor, who could nohow abide dirty stock.

But there was one prize piece in that old book which absolutely fitted more than one stupid Suffolk 'mor': '. . . even as a mother crys out against her child in her lap, when she calls it slut and naughty girl, and then falls to hugging and kissing it.' Suffolk women had a word for it, they called such children little 'mucks'!

This religious atmosphere pervaded the whole of the home, for beside the pantry door, between it and the backhouse door, was a sampler in a narrow little frame. It was the work of grandmother's own hand when she was being taught to sew, worked in coloured threads:

> Jesus, permit thy gracious name to stand
> As the first effort of an infant hand,
> And as her fingers on the canvas move
> Instruct her tender thoughts to seek thy love;
> With thy dear children let her have a part,
> And write thy name thyself upon her heart.

Then too, she had an old skillet with a long handle which had a text on it: 'Be strong!' She was never quite sure whether this referred to the skillet or her own moral standing. Mr. White, the rector, had gone one better than that, for when travelling abroad he had become possessed of an iron jamb-stove of German origin on which was another text: 'Watch and Pray.' He had brought it home and had it installed in his new rectory and called it his Iron Bible. His cook thought it was full of meaning!

Mr. White was rather fond of grandfather, and liked nothing better than a talk with him; also he was fond of a chat with grandmother, sitting in that turkey twill-covered chair and enjoying her fire. Since he had been set down, as it were, in such a richly endowed spot he loved to listen to any accounts of local lore that she could tell, for he used to say he had been taught of mysteries hidden from many professors in the cottages he had visited. And what was more, that the faith of the saints of all ages was the truth. That was why he felt so comfortable when he entered his own old, old church, and was why he secretly raised his hat when he drove past the ruins of Leiston Abbey, where the chapel was now a pig-sty and the graves of the monks lay under the cow-yard. He had to be careful about this action since his coachman, Jonah Barham, was another Methodist, and didn't hold with papists.

Grandfather was a local preacher, a job that was no sinecure in those days of wide circuits, but how and when he made his sermons I cannot say. They must have sprung from a bucolic ebullience, lacking book learning but fortified by common sense and a wide knowledge of Mother Earth. It was a small house and he was unlearned, but perhaps his sermons came to him in the fields, in which case they would be fresh, free from the smell of the lamp or carpet bag and, after all, it was an age of certainties. It might mean a ten- or twelve-mile walk there on a Sunday, preach twice and then foot the same miles back, though they had a knack of seeming longer on the return journey. Yet the preacher did it cheerfully for no reward, thought nothing of it in fact, and a good preacher such as grandfather was, had the inner satisfaction of knowing he was appreciated. Later there was a horse-hire fund, which provided them with a pony and trap, and they baited the old hoss at the inn.

Those old Methodists who were all members of the Church of England were sincere and enthusiastic Christians, for they had nothing to gain by their profession. If they were up against it, it was of no use applying to the rectory, or trying the *arly sarvice* to see if that would produce anything. They met in Class, sat round a man or woman Leader, who was that much wiser than they, talked about their souls' welfare, and their ultimate hopes of a Better Land, since for many this was none too good in spite of such a lovely setting. And they cheered themselves into a positive fervour by singing Charles Wesley's hymns, for he gave them 'Wrestling Jacob,' 'Jesu, Lover of my Soul,' 'Love divine all loves excelling,' 'Soldiers of Christ arise,' and many others to be found in hymnals of all denominations. It is true to say their meetings together made them better men and women, and filled their lives with a happiness that found expression in their faces.

Help us to help each other, Lord,
Each other's cross to bear;
Let each his friendly aid afford,
And feel his brother's care.
We all partake the joys of one,
The common peace we feel;
A peace to sensual minds unknown,
A joy unspeakable.

John Wesley was a romantic figure to them. He was a scholar, since he had come out of a country rectory, and had been to college. They were country folk, and they looked on this travelling preacher, whom some of their fathers had heard when he came that way, with the awe due to those who had 'got larnin'!' He was their man! Travelling on horseback, getting a snatch meal from the hedgerow, and dabbling in primitive medicine, and not so primitive, since he was a pioneer in electrical treatment: he may well have said: 'For more than twenty years I have had numberless proofs that regular physicians do exceedingly little good.'

John Wesley taught them much. Poor himself, he could speak to the poor, and he taught them to give. 'If you earn but three shillings a week and give a penny of it you will never want.' Neither did they, and that was the amount they gave each week when they met in Class, and doubled it each quarter when they met for Tickets. Tickets of membership which they treasured all their long lives; little rectangles of paper bearing a letter of the alphabet and a text, and their name in full written in by the minister. And when they came to die, amongst their treasures would be bundles of these little billets, tied up with tape, sere with age, save the recent ones. And not one would be missing!

There was a quality about John Wesley that appealed to grandfather, and that was his sound common sense. He would appreciate the religious fervour which said 'Join hands with God to make a good man live,' but in all probability he was quite unaware that those same lips spoke of gospel sermons, 'That term is now become a mere *cant* word.' And of some of his own preachers, '. . . three other persons, as *unlearned* as any of the Apostles, but I believe not *so much inspired*.'

In common with his neighbours grandfather was very poor, and a penny represented a good deal, but he was enterprising and thrifty. It has been said that thrift, patriotism and religion were outstanding virtues in Victorian times, which is true. But it was a shining thrift in my grandfather's case, leading on to giving and not to miserliness. Wesley had told them they would not want; and when he died my grandfather managed to leave a little nest egg for his children. Neither was his religion tinged with hypocrisy, but rather the dynamic force of his life. It was not a case of 'couldn't care less,' but rather 'couldn't care more!'

How Methodism came to grandfather's countryside I cannot say, but he could remember the services in the barns, lent by a sympathetic farmer. The congregation, as much akin to the Pilgrim Fathers as anything else, finding their way there across the footpaths, the women in poke bonnets, full skirts, and the men in their fustian. They met and sang, sitting round on sacks and farming implements, while the pulpit or rostrum would be a hay-wain such as Constable painted. Horn lanterns would give the light, and there would be that other Light. Then, when the weather was too bad, a farmhouse kitchen replaced the barn.

> Jesus, where'er Thy people meet,
> There they behold Thy mercy-seat;
> Where'er they seek Thee Thou art found,
> And every place is hallowed ground.

Pennies went a long way in Methodism, and soon in those

cottage homes, standing near to hand, were lovely little pottery collecting-boxes in the shape of a house (or was it a chapel?). Gaily coloured, out of some Staffordshire pottery, they shone with a gaiety not usually associated with religious conventicles, and simply invited pennies into their interiors. So their chapel was born. It is of red brick, a sort of Suffolk Spiritual, an honest-to-goodness piece of chapel architecture, and set in it is a little white stone with the date 1827.

Middleton was somewhat unique as an agrarian community since it had no direct squire, for he lived in the next parish of Theberton. That may explain in some measure why their chapel was relatively early in its origin, and why Nonconformism had such a hold. But it is equally true that the relationship between it and the parent church has always been of a cordial nature. The value of that little chapel to many a country heart can only be gauged when one realises that every brick and tile, plank and pillar, even every nail and screw was paid for out of their penurious pockets, a penny at a time. How they watched it grow! Sweat and blistered hands, made skilful by a great love, built that chapel.

There was another side to the chapel, for Wesley was no mere insular evangelist; had he not spent some time in the West Indies, and on the Continent in Georgia? Methodism therefore was a missionary church, and in those cottage homes was a Missionary Box of shining polished mahogany. The children made that their special interest, and any occasional coin collected by some lucky event such as opening a gate for some horse rider to pass through, went into its depths. To them it represented fascinating black people, distant lands and adventure:

> Where the grim satyr-faced baboon
> Sits railing to the rising moon;
> Or chiding, with hoarse angry cry
> The herdsman as he wanders by.

Behind the chapel, as one views it from the village green and the old pump (once such a centre of goings and comings, but now not used owing to the advent of piped water), is the churchyard, where

> At eve the beetle boometh
> Athwart the thicket lone:
> At noon the wild bee hummeth
> About the mossed headstone.

This is situated on a slight escarpment, accentuated by a narrow hill on the south side, and therefore takes to itself the nature of a keep, guarding the ancient dead Christians,

> There a very little girth
> Can hold what once the earth
> Seemed too narrow to contain.

Some lie under old leaning lichened stones with cherub heads, skulls and hour-glasses; others under mouldering grave-boards that look like the heads of truckle beds. Many have no memorials save those of turfed mounds spangled with primroses in spring time, once protected from browsing cattle by bonds cut from the male briar, spikes outwards. The churchyard is hemmed in by elms that not only lament in any wind, but become hoarsely vocal at night with screeching owls. Here somehow is yesterday, today, even tomorrow, peacefully resting until a trumpet sound shall rend it all into space and everlastingness.

The church is the oldest building in that old settlement, entered on the south side by a Norman doorway. It has a western tower, surmounted by a slender pricket of a spire, which is covered by lead shingles in the form of chevrons; and it shows its long history in mouldings and tracery. For example, there is a fine billet mould around the arch of the east window, and within is one of the prettiest and most unusual of piscinas dating, like the south doorway, from Norman times. Long after grandmother was dead a huge St. Christopher (the Child with a Flemish face) was discovered under the whitewash of the north wall. 'Ah!' said the old folk, who gazed on it with awe, 'reckon he be a comin' thro' Rackfur Run!' After all, their local stream was of the greatest importance to them.

At the services the old folk and the young men would shuffle into their places, making a deference to the Holy Table by touching their foreheads, while the women would curtsy. Often, too, by habit, the men would congregate in the churchyard, or at the gate, both before and after the service, discussing village affairs and the prospects of the crops. The men usually went into the church last as the bidding bell was about to cease.

The service would open with one of the versicles, the first phrase repeated thrice in increasing intensity: 'If we say we have no sin! If we say we have no sin!! If we say we have no sin!!! WE DECEIVE OURSELVES!' Mr. White preached in a black gown and wore black gloves that were too long in the fingers, so that when he emphasised a point— as so often he did—waving his hands produced a rather comic effect. When the custom came in of wearing a surplice during the sermon, old Betsy Backhouse confided to a friend —'Dew you know, Sarah, he never shiffen hisself once!'

It is perhaps not surprising that this old church and its services had given rise to a good many superstitions and customs. For instance, many a woman in the village believed that her husband had been 'lotted' to her, and that she knew it before he had ever spoken to her. Also, it was unlucky to hear one's banns called, since the first child might arrive deaf and dumb. Another custom was that of giving a bunch of white everlasting flowers to a bride elect by a matron who had been happily married. This was then given by the bride to her husband on the wedding day. It was thought to be a survival from the tournaments, and a sign of everlasting love.

Then there was a strange though picturesque custom of burying single persons, carrying the body on a sheet, by four men or four women according to sex. The men were dressed in white trousers and blue jackets, wearing white hats, while the women wore white dresses, white stockings, black shoes, black silk capes and white poke bonnets trimmed with plaited white muslin round the front edge which fell down to form strings. In some cases white towels were put under the coffin of a woman to carry by, and the women bearers wore a long white skirt hanging about a foot below the dress. A piece of white calico was drawn over the head to form a rough bonnet, the ends acting as strings which tied under the neck in a bow. They also wore white gloves. The men wore bowler hats, with a white cloth or towel tied round and the ends hanging behind.

Other customs concerned Funeral Cakes, or little loaves which were distributed at the funeral and sent to those who were unable to attend. In the case of funerals from the large houses, everyone who attended was presented with a hat-band, scarf and gloves.

Both grandfather and grandmother lie in that old church-yard, just under the skirting flint wall on the south side. It is a characteristic Suffolk flint wall with a rounded brick top, just right to lean upon and reflect. They have a Victorian gravestone to their memorial and instead of skulls, hour-glasses and cherubs, there are forget-me-nots and doves! Their son, lacking inspiration, indited the inscription, giving them a verse which states—

Fixed in this ground will I remain.

But that was spoken of the living, not of the dead, and had no reference to churchyard soil.

Not very far removed, in fact quite close, lies the Rev. Mr. White under a broken column. On a panel at the base his relict informs us that he died of a 'long and painful illness, unexpectedly, suddenly, and as it were accidentally.'

Then, skirting the path which leads to the south door, is the grave of Charles Godward, late of Her Majesty's 16th Lancers, who distinguished himself at the battles of Maharajpur, Alliwall, Buddawai and Sobraon.

Did they all stir in those quiet graves when the thatch on the church roof caught fire? I wonder!

THE COOL BRICK FLOOR

For freshest wits I know will soon be wearie
Of any book, how grave so e'er it be,
Except it have odd matter, strange and merrie,
Well sauc'd with lies and glared all with glee.

<><><><><><><><><><><><><><><><><><><><><><><><><>

NEITHER grandmother nor grandfather bathed themselves, they were not dirty because their faces and hands were the only nakedness they ever exhibited to the light of common day; so why should they? But then, no one had ever thought it necessary to bathe themselves, at least not as far back as they could remember. It may have been something to do with the mediaeval dislike of washing in water as being likely to bring on dangerous humours, but the fact remained it simply wasn't done. They washed their hands and faces in rain water, in a wooden tub set on a stool by the backhouse door, and sometimes bathed their feet in mustard and water to cure a cold. Even this last rash act was not resorted to often as it was a risky business, besides, they preferred dealing with a cold by other means, inwardly and more directly. The fact was they were mortally afraid of ague, and they would do anything to ward it off. They took tremendous care of both extremities, and seemed to leave the middle to take care of itself.

Certainly they would never think of washing their hair! Why, they would catch their death of cold! In fact grandmother's head was never uncovered, for she wore a cap in the house all day, and when she went to bed, took it off and put on another in which to sleep, the strings being tied under the chin in a bow. Likewise grandfather. True he took off his hat when he came in from the fields, leaving a high line of pale forehead, but when he went to bed, on went his nightcap. This may have been partly 'to keepe off the flies from pitching on the baldness.' Unkind later generations have said it was to keep the pillow-cases clean, but more probably it was to ward off draughts; and the curtains round the bed were to the same end, as also the smallness of the windows. Even when grandfather had his hair cut, he would hurry home and take a glass of hot elderberry wine, no matter what the time of year. As to his feet, he would cut off the feet of a pair of stockings and wrap his bare extremities in pieces of white linen or calico to prevent them becoming galled. And he shaved his round Hogarthian face once a week, regular, whether it wanted it or no, and his old cut-throat razor fairly sang as it ploughed through the stubble!

Yes, it was a serious affair this washing of feet, but sometimes dire necessity drove them to it. Poor old Polly Vincent, grandmother's witch-like neighbour, suffered with one of hers right bad; so there was nothing for it but to go and see 'Mr.' Bailey. It should be mentioned in passing, that he was the local doctor and lived at Yoxford, three good miles away, and was always referred to as 'Mister.' It was the horse doctor who was known as 'doctor.' So she drove off in her old dickey cart (a sort of homemade shandrydan), and hobbled into his snug old surgery.

'What's ailing o' you, Polly gal?' was his greeting.

'Well, that's like this 'ere, Mr. Bailey, I ha' gort suffen come to my fut. That's right bad, an' I don't fare to be able to lift it at all!'

'Off with your highlow then, Polly!' demanded Bailey.

With that Polly bent down her old seamed, pouched and puckered face with its rheumy squint, and proceeded to unlace her boots. It was something she had anticipated before she ventured on the journey. After a struggle off it came, a crinkled misshapen leather product of the cobbler and his last; and there was her foot with hammer toes, and gleaming white in striking contrast to her rubicund complexion. She stuck it out and held her breath!

Bailey leaned down, took the old foot in his hand and

tickled her under the instep to see if she reacted, but as Polly did not move an eyelid, he knew there was something wrong. He then felt carefully round her toe joints and the ankle to see if there was any swelling.

'How long have you been troubled this way, Polly?'

'Since afore Michaelmas, if I recollect rightly. That must have been about barley harvest, when I took my poor dear brother's wittals to him in the field over hinward. I fare to run a bush in my fut, an' that hain't bin right since!'

Bailey knew by that that instead of a whole bush Polly meant a thorn, and that hinward was over yonder, some-where to the east of her dwelling.

'Oh, did you bathe your foot?'

'Well, not exactly; I had a tissickin' cold at the time, an' I thowt that warn't wise.'

'Come then, Polly, take off that other highlow and let me see both feet together!'

This was greeted with a pause of some length, then slowly and deliberately. 'No, master, I 'ont do that. That's this fut what hurt, not its twin. T'other's all right!'

'But I must see it, Polly. I can't do anything for you unless I do.'

'Then I must be a going, master, for you certainly won't see it.' With which remark she put on her old boot and hobbled off as she had come. Bailey thought he heard a remark which sounded like: 'Duzzy owd fule!' but he only laughed. Arrived at the door Polly turned, and in the high sing-song of her county enquired if he, the doctor, would be near her home before long. Bailey said he would.

'Well, it's like this here, Mr. Bailey, I hain't washed this t'other foot, but if so be as you'll call I'll have that kinder ready for you time you do!'

How they got on for baths in the big houses was best known to themselves. True they spent large sums on Palladian ball-rooms and conservatories, but you never heard of them building a bathroom. In fact there wasn't one for miles around, but there were a lot of powdering closets as used by their ancestors. As the century progressed, however, there was a feeling after cleanliness and washing in bedrooms was the order of the day. For this a whole battery of baths were provided by the hardware man. There were hip baths, tray baths, sitz baths, foot baths and slipper baths; all finished in the same way, oak grained on the outside and plain white within. And these baths were personal, just as was one's napkin or nightshirt, so that when you travelled you took your bath with you, for lids were provided, with straps, and a wicker cage inside so that you could use the interior for part of your voluminous luggage. A peppery old colonel would have considered it a sacrilege if someone else bathed in his bath. There were even shower-baths on stilts, worked like a lavatory flush. You stood underneath, pulled the chain, and down came the rain, which had been carefully put in by the housemaid, using a water-can finished exactly like the baths. But the work involved in these bedroom ablutions was best known to the indoor staff, who had to pad the floor with towels, glue up the windows and doors, carry up and carry down the water.

But if they didn't wash their bodies they kept their linen clean, having a regular turn-out once a month. Ash from the ash-pit of the brick-oven came into use via the letch-bucket, which had turned it into a soft solvent very useful for the whites and dainty pieces of napery. On the day in question the copper fire was lit, and the wooden wash-tubs got out, while grandmother put on her pattens to keep her feet out of the slush. With these, too, she slipped in and out of the yard, hanging up the clothes. No scrubbing was allowed; they knew better than that, for grandmother's domestic training had been thorough and severe. The clothes were rubbed, using old primrose which she got in golden bars from the shop; and then lifting them out of the sudges the clothes were popped into the copper to be boiled up with any odd bits of soap that had been saved up for the purpose, for soda was not looked upon favourably. They were rinsed in three waters, the last containing blue, and then wrung out. For this the clothes were not just wisped up but pleated concertina fashion into convenient folds, and then wrung. To dry they were laid out on the grass or a hedge, which tended to give them a better colour. If they were hung, then it was on stout lines and held with funny little wooden pegs that grandmother bought from the cooper, since she did not like the gipsies' wares. These pegs were cut from solid billets, either of ash or hickory, no two of which seemed to be alike; and they lasted a lifetime.

Then came laundering before a clear fire, at which grandmother's armoury of box and sad irons, goffering irons and tongs were heated. She even made her own starch from old potatoes. These were grated under water and the resultant mash left for twenty-four hours. The dirty water was then strained off and the deposit set on a tray and dried. When ironed and folded, the clothes were laid in the brick-oven to air, before being put away in lavender or woodruff. No wonder everywhere smelt so sweet.

This was grandmother's method, but they did things differently at Dunwich. She knew because she had a sister-in-law who lived there. Westward of the newly built church was a holy well, the well of St. James, and the water from that well was used for their washing, and they did it on the spot in the open air. The water was soft and sparkling and came up from such a depth that it was said that if you put your hands in it it was so cold that it made your arms ache to the shoulders, even on the hottest day. And the women danced on the dirty clothes just as they did in Paris, on the banks of the Seine.

Grandmother brewed her beer, as did most of her neighbours, and her old and spicy brewing tackle was housed in a shed in the yard. She valued her casks and gear because they had belonged to her mother, and were mellow and ripe. Two main brewings in the year were her task, one in March for the hard work of haysel and harvest, and the other in October for Christmas. She preferred rain water to that from the pump, as it was softer. In the process of the brewing, before the hops were added, the liquid was known as sweet wort, and this was said to be good for diarrhoea. That was the time when the children were in evidence as they liked a glass of this rather sickly stuff. Sometimes she strewed brown sugar on the bottom of the tub, the effect of which was to darken the beer and assist fermentation.

Brewing was almost always done by women, and hard work it was, but they had that peculiar instinct of knowing what to do and when, which the men lacked. For example, the yeast or burgad had to be added at blood heat. How did the housewife know when this moment arrived, since she had no thermometer? She would sweep her old wrinkled hand through the liquid, ponder in her wise old country way, and say 'yes' or 'no' as the case might be. If it was 'yes' a pint was added, but if 'no,' she would remark: 'That's too hot, partner, the beer will bloom if we do that yet!'

After the beer had cooled, the yeast which floated on the top was skimmed off by a fleeter (the same instrument used to remove the cream from the milk), and put into stone bottles ready for baking, with a little clear water run in on top. The beer was then tunned into the casks by means of a wooden funnel (grandmother called it a tunnel), black with age and many a brew, and care had to be taken that the casks were not over-filled. The casks were then left a few days for the final working to take place and the surplus yeast removed as it came out through the bung-holes. When they were finally bunged, brown paper was pasted over the bung-holes and the wind peg or spigot loosened, otherwise there would have been an explosion. A comfortable feeling of satisfaction pervaded the small household when the barrels were snugly housed on the beer stools in the pantry or cellar, carefully wedged into their peaceful position. Beer had to be treated gently, and must not be riled on any account.

Baking day, which was on a Friday, was a weekly pleasure that filled the house with the nicest appetising smells that could be imagined, particularly so in keen frosty weather. What a smell to greet the nostrils on opening the door after a tramp through the fields, and how tantalising to a hungry stomach! No such aroma is left in the world today.

The dough was prepared the night before in a great earthenware pan, into which grandmother would empty a stone of flour, adding a little salt. Then she would make a crater in the middle and drop into the hole a spoonful of yeast mixed with a little lukewarm milk. The flour was gradually sprinkled on to this until the yeast was covered. Now some warm skim milk was added and the whole worked and kneaded by hand until the right consistency was gained. The dough was then covered over with a warm cloth and left to rise. She called this 'laying the sponge.' In poor households mashed potatoes were put in. Care had to be taken all through the process to see the dough was kept warm, to which end she placed the pan on the right side of the hearth, or on the copper if that had been in use. Although she was a staunch Protestant and a Methodist, she would seal her dough with the sign of the Cross.

When she began baking she would place the dough on the pastry board, cut it in portions and put them in the tins, slashing the dough across the top, making her own mark which she would never change, lest she changed her luck. But then it was unlucky to bake an odd number of loaves, or upset a loaf when putting in or taking out of the oven; and she would be very vexed because upsetting meant a death in the house.

Grandmother's bread was put in the oven last, and it was

done in one operation, so that the oven door once closed was not touched again lest the bread was sent sad or heavy (cf. sad-irons for the laundering). When the bread came out there was a scramble for the crisp crusts, or for a kissing crust, which was that between two cottage loaves joined together. These were baked on the floor of the oven, without tins. Sometimes she cooked a bannock or dannock, which was baked on the peel held in the oven. This was a piece of dough, presumably the last piece, mixed with brown sugar and raisins. It was a tit-bit for the children who were always hungry. As she used to say—

> Children and chicken
> Are always a' pickin'.

But there was a little bit more sometimes, when each child was very young. That last fragment of dough was fashioned into the shape of a doll, with currants dotted in for features. How little Ally delighted in this and clapped his hands! That was before he went off to the churchyard. Grandmother used to say that her mother had done exactly the same thing for her and her sisters and brothers, down there at Hog Corner.

The harvest-cake, or biscuit, called by some a bever-cake, was only made at that season. For this a portion of dough was taken off the bread and put in a basin, mixed with lard, two eggs, sugar, raisins, candied peel and nutmeg. This was all thoroughly mixed by hand and left for a time; then baked in a tin, either in biscuit form or as a slab.

Fatty-cake was yet another form, made from a lump of dough rolled out flat, then spread with lard, sprinkled over with sugar, and doubled over. This rolling out, larding, sugaring and doubling over was repeated several times before shaping the dough into a cake for the oven. These simple bulging-sided cakes, oozing with burnt sugar, were particularly toothsome as I very well know, since grandmother taught her daughters these tasty bits in cookery. Dough was also shortened down with lard to make crusts for chicken or meat pies.

Dumplings also came off the dough, pieces about the size of a small fist were broken off and boiled for twenty-five minutes in salted boiling water. They were excellent with rich gravy from the joint, thus: 'Baste the meat well with the dripping and about an hour before dinner put three-quarters of a cup of boiling water into the latchpan (latch = to catch what falls), dredge in some flour and keep basting every ten minutes. Five minutes before dinner add a little more boiling water if required and set the pan on the top of the stove when it will brown and thicken.'

There were also swimmers and floaters, made from the dough. These were rolled flat and cut into pieces the size of a tea saucer and the thickness of a crumpet. They were slid into boiling water, and served to take off the edge of an appetite, since they were eaten before the meat with treacle or sugar.

The order of procedure into the oven was first, the bread into the fierce heat. Sometimes this was done in one operation to avoid tampering with the oven door. Then followed sausage rolls, called 'fill bellies,' meat pies, fruit tarts, milk puddings, potato pudding (made of potatoes, slices of fat pork, onions, with or without a pastry crust. Very delicious for tea on baking days), beef puddings baked in batter and apples done likewise. And last of all shortcakes, tarts, buns, rusks and all small things. Grandmother's skill with the oven peel was remarkable, putting in the various things, edging them off into the glowing depths of the oven, and edging the peel under them again when cooked, and bringing them out without a mishap, all smoking hot. Moreover, she was careful to see that nothing was high-baked (over baked).

Yes, grandmother was worth knowing on a Friday, and oft-times a good dinner, or odd scraps, would be sent off by one of the girls to a deserving neighbour. The poorer they were, the more thankful. But there were some who were never satisfied, of whom grandfather would say, 'They're fooks where Self's ullus at home!' Or, more expansively, 'Do you know, Susannah, if that were to rain bread and milk, the next thing they'd want would be for it to rain a spoon!'

Grandmother kept bees, those other-worldly creatures that must not be bought with money, must be told of a death in the family, 'tinged' home [attracted by a tinkling sound] when they swarmed and sometimes destroyed to get the honey. Neither must there be any strife in the house or they would not thrive. They were housed in bee skeps of the inverted extinguisher type, made of wheaten straw bands, laced together with thongs of briar and topped with flat red earthenware dishes. There was a rhyme about bees and grandmother's girls laughed when they came to the end:

A swarm of bees in May is worth a load of hay;
A swarm of bees in June is worth a silver spoon;
A swarm of bees in July isn't worth a fly;
A swarm of bees in August is worth a load of sawdust.
A swarm of bees in September is something to remember;
A swarm of bees in October is rare if one is sober;
A swarm of bees in November resembles one in December.

Another version of the May swarm was it was worth a mare's foal. Grandmother would drape their hives in black in the event of a death and cover them up with a white sheet when they swarmed and were safely back in their hives.

Her mead was strong stuff, enough to send home the bees themselves in a state, let alone the humans who took a full glass. Here is her recipe: 'Put $2\frac{1}{4}$ lbs. honey to a wine gallon of water; before you use the honey, see the depth of the water in the copper by putting in a stick, upon which cut a notch at the place where the surface of the water comes up to—then put in the honey and boil the liquor down to the said notch of the stick, put in some races of ginger to boil with it, when it is almost cold in the cooler put in a toast of bread spread thin with yeast, cover it, and let it stand two days before it is cask'd, when put in two cut lemons and a quart or two of brandy, according to the quantity.' It must have been good!

But her wines were wonderful. Cowslip or paigle, which she said was good for the memory, and the one thing that would make a new-born foal suck. It was a lovely amber colour and beaded; a glassful filled the room with scents from the hedgerow. Then there were champagne rhubarb, colts-foot, parsnip, sloe (the womenfolk used to laugh and say it was 'sloe-hatching time' when the white blossoms appeared on the blackthorns, and it was so wonderful cold). Black-currant (with which she dosed a 'tissicking' cold) and white-currant from a bush near the pump in the yard that bore clusters as large as grapes. Raisin, and gooseberry wine that might burst the bottles; dandelion, that was of great benefit; blackberry, and elderberry, used as a nightcap and as good as an extra blanket on the bed if taken hot or laced with gin. And here in passing is a recipe for elderberry wine: 'A bushel each of elderberries, blackberries and sloes, with loaf sugar—not coarse moist—according to taste. To be taken hot or cold.' In fact she could distil from almost any fruit or way-side plant that grew, not forgetting the crab-apple juice or verjuice, one of the cleanest, sharpest and most aromatic of the distillations. This provided a gargle for sore throats, and a compress for inflamed cuts or wounds.

To end this chapter, here are some of grandmother's recipes—beginning with the favourite, cowslip, always such a welcome visitor with its attendant Early Purple Orchid.

'Pick your cowslips [she called the petals 'blows'], to every pound of Flowers take a Gallon of Water, and beat the Flowers in a Marble Mortar: then mix them with the Water, to every six Gallons of Water add a Dozen of Seville Oranges, squeeze in their Juice, let six of their Skins be put in with the Juice, and let it stand all Night in the Tub, then strain them through a Sieve; to every Gallon of Liquor add four pounds of double-refined Sugar, and stir well together; add two Spoonfuls of Gile-yeast [Gile, an old name for Ale], and let it stand all Night in the Tub; turn it into a cask, adding a pint of Brandy to every six Gallons of Wine, bung it down close, leaving the Spile in the hole open till it be done working; then close it up, and in six Months' Time you may bottle it.'

Rhubarb Wine: 'To every gallon of cold water, rain water is best, add 5 lbs. ripe rhubarb cut in very thin slices, let it stand nine days not failing to stir it three times a day, and cover it over with a rug or blanket, then strain it and squeeze the substance through a coarse cloth. To every gallon of the liquor add 4 lbs. of white sugar, the juice and rind of 2 lemons, then to fine it one ounce of Isinglass to every 9 gallons. Take about a pint of the liquor in a saucepan to melt the isinglass over a slow fire. Be sure it is cold before you turn it back to the other, then cask it, and when the fermentation is over bung it down, then bottle it next March.'

Gooseberry Wine: 'To 1 gallon of bruised fruit ½ gall. of water, let them remain in the water 48 hours and squeeze them through a cloth; to each gallon of liquor add 4 lbs. of Lisbon sugar, let it stand 24 hours, put it in the cask and when it has done hissing stop it down.'

Then this for a cough, which seems better than that provided by the Health Service. 'One tablespoonful of honey, do. salad oil, 1 new egg, juice of a lemon, ½ wine glass of rum.'

Yorkshire Pudding: 'See that the batter is well mixed and beaten up in a basin; then poured into a large square heated pan, and partly cooked in the oven. It should be finished off in front of the fire by being placed under the joint cooking on the spit, and soaking up the rich gravy.'

THUS, THUS, AND THUS,
WE COMPASS ROUND
Herrick

Scythes tinkle in each grassy dell,
Where solitude was wont to dwell.
Clare

❖◇❖◇❖◇❖◇❖◇❖◇❖◇❖◇❖◇❖◇❖◇❖◇❖◇❖◇❖◇❖◇❖◇❖◇❖◇

FARMING in those early years of last century had changed but little. The very flail which grandfather wielded with such dexterity on the barn floor after harvest was portrayed in a stone carving on the ancient font in his church, with other memorials of the seasons. It was enough for him that his whole life, and his auburn setting was Biblical through and through, with the Squire as his Patriarch, absolute in his domain since he was a magistrate and ran the Home Farm, which kept and maintained a stallion, a bull and a boar. That was as it should be, completing and securing the family scheme. It was further sanctified in that lovely custom observed in drilling a field, when the head carter would take off his hat and say the grace, 'May God send us luck!' Again, when the sowing was finished, in like manner, 'With God's blessing may we have a crop!'

It is perhaps difficult for us to visualise, or even understand, the conditions and customs that prevailed when grandfather followed the calling of a husbandman. We know the seasons well enough with their inexorable chain of causation, from Plough Monday to Horkey; when the yellow tassels shook on the shining saplings, until the 'season of mists and mellow fruitfulness.' But how those fields were tilled and those harvests reaped is another story, and the record for us today is almost fantastic. A revolution had been in progress since Jethro Tull first evolved his drills on his farm at Wallingford in 1700, and Townsend his turnips, but the tempo has moved beyond all reckoning in these last few years. If grandfather could return and watch his acres being tilled now, see the result of a sound mechanisation policy, balanced stocking, improved drainage on the marshes and irrigation of the light land, he would make but one exclamation, 'Lawks a mussy! It's contrary to natur',' which for him would be as good as saying that it was going against the Lord. But he would without doubt suffer moments of envy when it came to the tally of bushels per acre. That would 'whooly stam' him!'

Labour was by hand, guided by a sure eye and a deep knowledge, working to an ancient pattern; and it was based on the four-course system then in vogue—turnips or mangolds, barley, clover, wheat or oats. By this hand-labour a man came into personal relationship with the soil until he knew and appreciated every inch and peculiarity of his native acres. Grandfather knew the difference between the Mardle Piece and Great Packway, and entered into the achievements of the Winding Field when it came to the reckoning, or the scanty crop snatched from Hungry Hill. He knew because he had ploughed up and down the furrows behind his team, calling to Bowler and Darkcy to 'cuppcy-whei!' or 'wheesh ho!' as he pulled his gallows plough to right or left, watching all unconsciously the nacreous light and the nuance of shade on the bare fields and the rain-wet trees.

Heavy land in those days was ploughed up in stetches of ten or twelve furrows in width, and the harrows, drills, rollers and horse hoes were made to fit these ridges. The horses walked in single file in the water furrow. This system was not necessary on the lighter lands which drained themselves. Sometimes, even now, these old stetches can be detected under grass, but cases are extremely rare.

A labourer would reckon his career by the number of harvests he had helped to garner with the scythe or sickle, it might be anything between sixty and eighty. And proud would he be as he told his tale. Forking sheaves was considered the hardest work and could only be done by the strongest men in the prime of life. This was rivalled by tossing hay or mowing grass; but stamina was not wanting even in the oldest, sustained by the home-brew lying cool and sheltered in a nearby holl (dry ditch). The wheat was often reaped with a sickle, and the stubble or haulm chopped with a scythe. This stubble formed one of the component parts of potash, and may well have given rise to the various Potash Farms. And these old men could cut an acre a day if it stood well.

It must be recalled of those years now so far away and long ago, that there was practically no machinery. When machinery did come it was looked at askance by the old hands, who realised, subconsciously, it is true, that the intimate individualist association of such ancient standing with the land of their heritage must inevitably pass. When steam ploughs capable of drawing as many as eight furrows at once, controlled by bearded men wearing peaked engineering caps, appeared in the fields they considered it a change for the worse; neither did they find any joy in following the first reaping machines which only cut and did not bind. For them the heart had gone out of the business, as also the musical chink-chink of the whetstone on gleaming steel. It was outside their conception to enter into the easing of the burden, for their work had never been a drudgery to them, but rather a way of life, with plenty of variations. The shepherd would sleep with his sheep, he and his dog; the horseman with the horses, and there might be as many as twenty of them, with almost half their number brood mares; and the cowman with the cows, as and when required.

The small one-horsed farms certainly possessed no machinery. Their stock-in-trade consisted of two or three flails, one or two wooden ploughs, a roll or roller, an improvised harrow, dibbling irons, various scythes and hooks, one of which would be a bramble scythe which had a short stout blade with a point bent downwards, and a handle with two jacks, and a hand chaff-cutter for the stable. The rolling stock might be one of those lovely wains or landships with a decorated headboard, and more than likely a 'morphadite' wagon. This latter was neither a wagon nor a wain as the name suggests, but was a cart with a forward attachment, that when in use provided two loading platforms and was most useful in haysel and harvest. There was also an herma-phrodite drill and scarifier in existence, but I doubt if this would have been seen on a small farm. This was really two implements with only one pair of wheels, as the drill box could be removed from its frame and a scarifier attached.

Perhaps one in the community possessed a drill, which he would take round to his neighbours, the fee being about 10s. a day and board for the use of the machine, and so much an acre for the work. Dibbling-irons were very popular for the sowing of corn and beans and cost 10s. a pair and about 8s. an acre in operation. They were economical with the seed since the requisite number of grains was dropped into the holes by the droppers. The latter in grandfather's case were his own children who were taught how to do this. Rebecca became quite an adept, and in later years would laugh and repeat the ditty as she showed the movement of the thumb over the fingers to allow the grain to fall out of the cupped hands:

> Four seeds in the hole,
> One to rot and one to grow,
> One for the rook and one for the crow.

In those days many horse and cow yards had no walls, but fences were made of haulms, which after two or three years became manure. One feature of the fields then was the clay pits from which was dug the clay used on newly broken up pasture land. Clay was also used for making farmyard walls. It was first made into a bed, covered over with straw, and well watered. Two horses were then made to tread it down, after which it was ready to be built into walls, using sticks from good faggots as risers, or it was made into bricks 18 inches long by 10 inches wide by 10 inches deep.

The cows were often kept out all night, the servants going out to milk them between four and five o'clock in the morning. They found shelter under the tall thick hedges round the fields, which had wide margins of grass bordering them. On these fences, as the hedges are still called by old people in Suffolk, would be hung the cows' fodder, and also straw to provide protection from wind and weather. The cows were timed to calve in the autumn, the object being to obtain a winter butter dairy. This delectable produce was sold in the village, or failing that taken to market. Cleanliness was the order of the day in those old pammet floor dairies and the skim milk was fed to the calves.

Reverting to the old wooden plough, which had not altered greatly from its Saxon counterpart and the one that was dragged to church for Plough Sunday, it had two wooden breasts, the one handle of which reached the ground. A bar of iron about half an inch thick and about 9 inches to 10 inches broad, cut to the proper width, was bent into shape to fit the breast. The shares were made of hammered iron and cost 2s. 6d. each. As these ploughs were highly individual and made to measure, the old weather-boarded blacksmith's shop on the Green, kept by Spall, had twenty to thirty of these shares hanging on its walls belonging to different farmers. The Tom Plough differed from the above by possessing only one wooden breast, each side being alike, with two handles instead of one. It was used to clean out the furrows that had been worked in by the process of drilling and harrowing. This facilitated the running away of the water from the land sown with wheat during the winter, and that sown with barley in the spring.

Grandfather rather favoured the old gallows plough, which had two wheels, a small wheel that ran on the land and a large wheel that ran in the bottom of the furrow. He always said it did a smooth clean job; and by changing the position of the mould-board at the end of the furrow it was possible for him to return down the same furrow and thus finish the work quicker. This plough was a bit of a novelty then, and he had a lot of folks come and want to know all about it.

Few farmers then had scarifiers or cromes to prepare the land for planting, so they used a gang of harrows with broad sharp blades, called teeth. These cut the land to pieces but would not raise the grass to the surface that it might die. Rather the grass was cut into small pieces, some of which would grow. A harrow would be made by a gate lashed through the ledges with whitethorn or blackthorn bushes. To this was attached a whipple-tree by which a horse was harnessed. The roller had no shafts, only staples, one at each corner, to which chains were attached to the collar of the horse. The frame of this would go up and down according to the looseness or otherwise of the chains. There were no horse hoes, and the work was done by hand, with hoes just as wide as the space between the ridges of corn. Heavy clay land was often broken up by the mattock, just as it had been treated in the days when the Luttrell Psalter was illuminated.

Drainage, which was done by hand, was either bush or pipe, the trenches being dug by those strange-looking wedge-shaped spades. This was the work of a specialist, who could also do bottom fyeing of the ditches (cleaning them out) and the laying of hedges. A peculiarly shaped implement was used in draining for scooping out the soil from the bottom of the channel which had been cut by the spade.

Grandfather's chaff-cutter was a home-made contraption, like so many of the other implements. It consisted of a long narrow shallow box, like a wooden trough on a stand, and was fed by a man with a short-handled four-tined fork. He would push the hay towards the knife which was fashioned from an old scythe-blade. At the front of the box was a square piece of wood which acted as a press upon the feed. This was attached to a lever, and upon it grandfather placed his left foot, and every time he pushed the feed with his fork he pressed his foot. The knife then cut the feed, up went the press again, propelled by the spring underneath the box, and thus room was made for more feed to pass on to the knife.

Neither were there any root cutters or pulpers other than those shaped like vertical foot scrapers, which were used chopper fashion. Grandfather used a four-legged stool, like a hurdle-maker's trestle, and at the end a peculiarly shaped long-handled knife was bolted upright. With this the roots were cut small and mixed in the manger with the chaff.

Of the rolling stock, the Quarter Cart might be mentioned. The name had nothing to do with its capacity, but referred to its construction. The shafts were not put in the middle but near the driving side, leaving a large space on the near side of the horse. It got its name from the quarters in the road, which were the spaces between the wheel-ruts and the horse path in the middle of the road, and when the shafts were so placed the horse of necessity had to walk or trot on the 'quarter.' These were light carts, the wheels of which were shod with strakes, as the old gigs used to be.

It should be remembered there was a tax on carts and gigs with steel springs in those days, so a coach-builder in the nearby market town of Framlingham rose to the occasion. He made and patented a lance-wood spring constructed of thin plates of wood, just like the steel springs, fastened together in the same way, and adjusted to a gig or cart as required. It was a wonderful bit of evasion.

The Suffolk Punch which gained a world-wide fame in its heyday, and was a marked feature of the London streets in the days of horse-drawn carriers' vans, was to be found on every Suffolk farm. Curiously enough its origins and name have become obscure. One source attributes the name to its round punchy make, but there is another contained in the privately printed *Punchard of Heanton-Punchardon: Records of an Unfortunate Family* (1894) written by the Rev. Elgood George Punchard, D.D. His great-grandfather, John Punchard, was a native of Saxtead, near Framlingham, and he writes of him thus, 'Not content with his own lands, he hired several farms including that of Parham Hall, and did much to improve the breed of horses and cattle. His red Suffolks known as "punches"—a corruption really of Punchard—became famous for their strength and beauty, and were victorious in all the drawing matches of the district. But a good deal of money was lost in these efforts and John Punchard died comparatively young in 1787.'

Harvest was the great occasion of the year towards which all work and achievement turned, and the men entered into an agreement with the farmer on Whit Monday to do the work for £6 per head, and a pair of gloves, priced seven-pence. It might seem strange today that the latter should figure as part of the payment, but it was a very old custom and these customs were so often based on usefulness. The bane of the harvest-fields was thistles, and since much seed was sown broadcast there was no room between the plants to do any hoeing. Besides, thistles had to be grubbed out, it was of little use to cut them down, hence the old pronged spuds that hung up in the shed. A farmer or a squire would never think of walking in his fields without carrying a spud. A term of contempt for a badly kept field then often heard was, 'That's a good graze for an owd dickey!' Of course the children had a rhyme for this,

> Thistle cut in May
> Come up again next day;
> Thistle cut in June
> Come up again soon;
> Thistle cut in July
> Will be sure to die.

Therefore these gloves were very useful to guard the hands of the labourers against them.

When harvest began the men would assemble at five in the morning to the sound of a tin horn blown by the Lord or head man of the company, for the dew drinking. If they were late they were not entitled to have old beer, which had been brewed in March for the occasion. They took good care to be in time, however, for the beer was worth having. This horn was also blown at breakfast, elevenses, dinner and fourses. At the latter they ate a special cake baked by the farmer's wife, known as 'Fourses Cake.' It was the size of a common dumpling and heavily studded with raisins. Often this was crumbled into a basin and the old beer poured over it. Much beer was consumed during these strenuous days and this was served from a ranter, which was a copper or brass can with a long handle as used in wine cellars. 'Fill up the Ranter!' was the great cry as they held up their old coloured ringed mugs for a fresh supply. I can well remember how pretty and countrified these looked in grandmother's pantry, some with a feather on the central ring.

Oat harvest came first, to be followed by wheat and barley, and at the conclusion of the wheat harvest there would be a dinner of roast beef and plum pudding at the farm, but the Horkey or Harvest Frolic came later. For this the Lord would visit local tradesmen and neighbours to solicit contributions, and the celebration would be held in the barn. Then the old toasts would be sung and the Master and Mistress duly honoured. Poor old Charlie Chambers who lingered long over the meat course because he was naturally a slow eater, was fearful lest he should miss the pudding, and as in any case he could not eat it hot, he usually made a pathetic adenoidal request (since his mouth was full), as to whether he could 'lay a piece a couldin'?' A great deal of work fell on the women on these occasions, baking the great joints in the old brick ovens or roasting them on a spit before the fire; boiling the plum-puddings in the great coppers, and the vegetables in pots hung on the hake over the great open hearths.

'Calling the Largesse' was another very old custom peculiar to grandfather's fields. Largesse was a toll extracted from strangers who set foot in the harvest field. Upon receipt of the gift the whole troop would gather in a circle and cry out, 'Holla! Largesse! Holla! Largesse!' They then set up two violent screams which were succeeded by loud vociferations, continued as long as their breath would serve, dying gradually away. It must have sounded very weird. The money so gathered was spent at yet another frolic, this time held at the pub.

These men had gargantuan appetites, not to be wondered at if we recall their work. Perhaps they thought that the more they ate the better they were paid, but if we consider how poor was their fare at other times, it was not surprising if they took full advantage of the spread before them.

The harvest gathered, work now concentrated about the barn where more improvised equipment was to be found. Few had thrashing or dressing machines, so after the corn had been thrashed by the flail it went through a process known as casting. A barn-tilt would be suspended to one side of the barn and the corn to be dressed heaped up, allowing several yards between it and the tilt. A man with a wooden shovel (cut out of one piece of wood, without join) would throw up the corn as high as possible against the tilt. In so doing the chaff would fall away from the ears on to the space between. Then another man with a sack over his head and another down his back would sweep up the chobs or chobbings away from the bank of corn at either end with a besom or birch broom, and the corn itself would be placed in sacks ready for the market.

Hand sieves were then much in use; for instance there was a sifting horse or sieve horse which cost 10s. and another to sift chobs from the wheat costing about 4s. Another was called a 'caving sieve,' with large mesh made of split willow, into which the corn and coulder was placed. The corn went through whilst all the short splinters of straw remained in the sieve. These cost 5s. 6d. The sifting horse and the latter kind of sieve were also used to dress seed such as clover, the cob being put in the caving sieve, when the seed would fall through.

There was also a winnower which was made with a 6-foot barrel, to the end of which were attached cross-pieces of wood. From these four splines were fastened lengthwise and to them four pieces of cloth, canvas or tilting were attached, 2 feet deep. The whole was mounted on an axle, provided with a handle, which, when turned, made the canvas flap, causing sufficient draught to free the light cosh from the seed, as it fell from the sieve to the floor. This cost as much as 20s.

Then there was a barn fan, which was made of osiers, and was 3 or 4 feet wide. This acted as a substitute for the winnower and was used for dressing small quantities of seed and grain. A man would partly fill it with undressed corn, and by holding the handle each side, would fan away the chaff from the corn, rolling it from side to side. By this action the chobs would get on top and be swept away with a goose wing. The barley was trodden by a horse to free it of the chaff; chopping it also with a broad iron scuppit (spade) made for the purpose by the blacksmith, or a hummeller was used, which was a light iron roller comprising blades of metal set edgewise.

There were always accidents in the harvest field, since someone could be relied upon to run a two-tined pitchfork into his leg or hand, fall off a loaded wagon and break a leg, be run over or get his foot mangled. That had been the case with Harriet Marjoram's husband, James. He cut his leg with a scythe, gangrene set in, and that was the end of him. And so he left Harriet a widow, round about the 'thirties with a tribe of children, to fend for herself and bring them up as respectable members of society. And she did, slaving away all the hours of daylight, the children turning out a credit to herself and her village.

Grandfather would never work with his shirtsleeves rolled up. His bare arms might get blistered and blood poisoning ensue. Neither would farmers hereabouts allow the women-folk to work in the fields with their gowns on. They had to take them off and work in their shifts. That sort of condition was readily complied with by Harriet, who had only one gown, and was never likely to have another. So she took it off, folded it up, patches and all. All the same, it was a happy time for everybody, especially the children. They were never too young or too small to do a job or earn a few coppers which went to the family budget. Their chief efforts were at gleaning, at which they became adepts:

> Wheat, wheat, Harvest Home!
> See what great bundles we bring home.

The younger members might gather enough corn to provide themselves with a new pair of boots, which, with care, would last them until next harvest. At least, Harriet saw to it that her children's did. If during the year she found any of her gals 'kicking out their highlows a playin' o' games,' then their pink dimpled bottoms paid the penalty. Between them, as a family, they would get as much as six to eight bushels of corn, which was a most valuable addition to their granary.

In those days of often great hardship, a country boy would start work at five years of age. One of Harriet's boys did, poor little mite! He was put to bird scaring, and as he was small, provided with a wheelbarrow to stand on to make himself more conspicuous, and a straw pent-house in the hedge in case of a tempest. How proud he was of the few coppers he took home each week, and how thankful Harriet was for them. Up at 4.30 each morning in the summer, walking three miles to his job, and never late. Wages were 7s., 8s., or 9s. per week for the men, with a taking harvest of £6, usually a month long. Women could earn 6d., 8d., or 10d. a day stone-picking, gavelling barley or harvesting, with their children running up as much as 3d. a day. Some of the children would be so young that they had to be carried to work, and would crawl on hands and knees amongst the turnips picking out 'gralick' (charlock).

There used to be a rhyme about children in those days,

> When you've got one you can run!
> When you've got two you can go!
> But when you've got three
> You must bide where you be!

Harriet used to say that was all squit! She had got far more than three. 'Bide where you be,' indeed! If she had done that, meaning at home, they would all have starved! So she struck out and carried on. True they had little or no meat, bread, butter or lard, but an onion served for dinner, hot potatoes and a turnip mashed together for tea, boiled potatoes, turnip, bread and broth made of potato water for Sunday's dinner, with dumplings and flet cheese added. The latter was so hard that it became known as 'Thump!' Do you wonder they ate and ate when it came to a Harvest Frolic, as indeed a Frolic it was?

Ploughing with oxen was usual in grandfather's time, although it was beginning to fade out after its long survival from Roman and Saxon times. These patient beasts were considered the best for poorly drained fields though they were slow in action. However, they kept on with a steady persistency, accomplishing an acre and a half a day, which was as much as a team of horses could do, but they were cheaper. They wanted plenty of room at the headlands as

Cockfield Hall, Suffolk

Yoxford, Suffolk

A company of quoit players outside *The Griffin*, Brockford

Outside *The Bull*, Bacton, nr. Stowmarket

they took a wide turn, and ground which had been worked by them was notable for the long curve at the ends. Then for draught purposes they were unequalled by reason of a long steady pull without a jerk. Mrs. Ogilvie (who was a country counterpart of Queen Victoria) maintained on her lands at Snape and Sizewell a number of oxen, and was the last landowner about these parts to use them.

Oxen differed from horses particularly in their furniture, being yoked by large ungainly wooden ox-yokes that were made by the cooper. (One remained in grandfather's barn, of faded pink like the undercarriage of the farm carts, lashed to a tie beam.) They differed again in the matter of shoeing, a process they disliked intensely. For this they were thrown, or if not, fastened in the horse-stocks, one of which stood until it tumbled to pieces just by the blacksmith's shop on the Green. The oxtips or queues, which were in two parts owing to the cloven hoof, were fastened on with nails that had been dipped into pork fat. This shoeing was necessary for stony soil, but they often went unshod for soft soil. Their collars were hinged, so that these could be opened to go over the horns when harnessing up; and their horns were often decorated with brass knobs, rendered necessary to prevent injury to other members of the team. These knobs were screwed on to the horns. It was often necessary to fit a nose net to prevent grazing whilst at work. A goad replaced the whip, which consisted of a long hazel stick with a piece of wire in the tip. If well fed with chaff and cavings from the thrashing floor, oxen responded nobly, but when turned for home they would express their pleasure in no uncertain manner, literally skipping and playing along the road, jingling their chains in sheer delight.

Outbreaks of pestilence loomed large in grandfather's time, but the treatment was not so drastic as now. They had their own way with animals, for they vaccinated calves against the garget, and if a pig fell ill its tail was cut off, or ears split;

to change the blood, so they said. Sometimes an incision was made behind the ear, close to the head, and a little peg of hellebore inserted. There was a dreadful occurrence of sheep rot one year when the liver-fluke attacked whole flocks, killing off the sheep by the score. This was traced to the sheep eating certain snails and swallowing the live grub, which found sustenance on the liver. Cattle disease was notified by placing the skull of an ox, impaled on a stake, at the entrance to the village as a warning. Grandfather had even heard of the Need Fire, when cattle so affected were passed through the smoke of the fires, which had been kindled by rubbing two pieces of wood together, when all the house fires had been extinguished. However, most of the village community dosed their cattle with Stockholm tar for such trouble, and hoped for the best. The cow leech was fetched as and when required, but the horse doctor came in his own gig. These were the medicines to be had, viz. black and red drinks, alternative powders, ewe drenches, foot rot oils, husk draughts for husk in horse or sheep, lambs and calves; and carminative chalk.

Fields were dressed with lime and phosphates and a feature of some farms was the chalk-drawing and lime burning. Coprolites were another dressing discovered about this time. This fossilised excrement of ancient animals had been discovered near the coastal regions of the red crag, and women and children were set to picking these stone-like objects from the fields. Coprolites were also raised from pits, and washed, then taken to a mill and crushed. One of the Darsham mills was used for this purpose. They were also shipped to London and used at the experimental station at Rothamsted, having been discovered by a Suffolk parson, the Rev. Professor J. S. Henslow, whilst on holiday at Felixstowe in 1843, in the crag cliff there.

Both grandparents had cause to remember this peculiar and most effective dressing, for grandmother's nephews, two young men, pulled up their roots and migrated to King's Lynn, a thing unheard of, and literally made their fortunes in artificial manures. However, they never forgot the old home and rejoiced in any opportunity of returning to their early scenes.

As grandfather lived so near the coast, he remembered the old salt-pans at work. The sea water was pumped into pans, or shallow square pits dug in the earth. It was then exposed to the sun until its freshness evaporated, leaving it seven times stronger than in the natural state. It was then pumped into flat iron pans, eight to ten feet square and as many inches deep, and boiled over a fierce fire until nothing was left but the pure salt.

Most of grandfather's co-labourers wore smocks. They were decorated with those exquisite specimens of stitchcraft denoting the wearer's calling as a husbandman. He could remember when these were woven by the womenfolk in the cottage homesteads, of flax that had been grown in garden or field, retted by these same housewives, and spun into a web by their own firesides. Indeed, in his young days it had been the custom in farmhouses for the servants to be so occupied at certain periods. Needless to say, grandmother could always tell a piece of linen from a piece of cotton, because if she wetted the tip of her finger with spittle and put it on the cloth, if it was linen it would 'spot' right through!

And so the year revolved and their life lived from day to day, uneventfully, quietly, yet always with a forward look, since their ending of the day was a preparation for the morning.

VILLAGE COMPANIES

'You played that very well, John Noble!'
'I know't, my lord, I know't.'

'The Helmingham Wolunteers,' raised by Lord Dysart to repel Bonaparte. John Noble was the drummer, afterwards wheelwright at Monk Soham. The above was said after a drill.

⟡⟡⟡⟡⟡⟡⟡⟡⟡⟡⟡⟡⟡⟡⟡⟡⟡⟡⟡⟡⟡⟡⟡⟡⟡⟡⟡⟡⟡⟡⟡⟡⟡⟡

ONE quality that characterised village life, as I have already stated, was its clannishness. This was evidenced in no small degree by the various Companies which existed, for both work and play, carrying on the tradition and spirit from one generation to another of that compact and self-supporting unit. It is true some of these were visiting bands, but for the most part they were of purely local recruitment, son joining father as time advanced; and there was always a Captain at their head. Moreover, they were known as Companies, since their occasions were lawful, and not gangs, such as those of smugglers and poachers. In all fairness, however, it must be mentioned that the Beach Companies to be then found strung along the coast, although forerunners of the Life Boat Service, had a somewhat doubtful reputation. Yarmouth had seven Companies, Lowestoft three, and Southwold, Aldeburgh, Orford and Thorpe probably one apiece. And this is what Crabbe said of the Aldeburgh Company:

'a bold, artful, surly, savage race;
Who only skill'd to take the finny tribe,
The yearly dinner, or septennial bribe,
Wait on the shore, and, as the waves run high,
On the toss'd vessel bend their eager eye;
Which to their coast directs its vent'rous way,
Theirs, or the ocean's miserable prey.

Each Company possessed gigs and yawls, and there was a race to get to the distressed ship first, rather because of the cargo than the lives of the seamen. Nall, the Yarmouth historian, said the children of beachmen had but one prayer, 'Pray, God, send Daddy a good ship ashore before morning!' Their old wooden huts, always a feature of the beaches where they plied, were decorated with figure-heads and name-boards of wrecks. Steam tugs put them out of business.

First we might consider the Company of Ringers, which was staffed mainly from local tradesmen, son often succeeding the father at a particular rope. They operated in the ringing chamber, which was the solar of the parish belfry, and their exploits are recorded on the dusty old steeple-boards still to be found in these towers. One of these boards in grandfather's county has the insignia of the ringer's trade placed beside each name. Number one was a bricklayer and has a trowel for his sign. Two and five were blacksmiths, so they have an anvil. Three and four were field workers, either drainers or hedgers and ditchers, so they are given a wedge-shaped spade such as is used in drainage work. Six was a shoemaker, and he has an extremely large awl, which brings to mind the East Anglian name for the avocet—the shoemaker's awl. One tower in the county had a clock, but the face was inside, for the benefit of the ringers.

This represents an ordinary small village community, and although there was but one bricklayer there were two black-smiths. Most villages had more than one of these, for at Middleton there were two; Samuel Martin Spall in the Street, and another on the turnpike, colloquially known as 'up by Title,' one Robert Foulsham, who was also a wheelwright. And there were four carpenters: John Larter, Henry Matkin, Samuel Mayhew and Jesse Merrells, who was also a builder.

As ringing was a thirsty job they would probably have a large stoneware pitcher or gotch amongst their possessions—

> Seven strong men to ring with ye
> And a strong boy to fetch the beer.

The gotch was usually inscribed, and was placed in the centre of the ringing chamber. More often than not it was the gift of an old member. One of these which holds sixteen quarts bears this admonition:

> If you love me Do not lend me
> Use me Often, and Keep me Clenly,
> Fill me Full, or Not at All,
> If it be Strong, and Not with Small.

The use of the capitals is not without significance. Sometimes these jugs were carried in procession through the village on special ringing occasions, when the ringers would solicit alms with which to fill them. The contents would be Old William, or some other strong brew, usually supplied by the landlord of the inn, who more than likely would be a ringer, and in his house the jug would rest when not on duty.

Grandfather's church has five bells, one of which, dated 1779, is inscribed:

> In Wedlock's bands all ye who join
> With hands and hearts unite
> So shall our tuneful tongues combine
> To laud the nuptial rite.

That their tongues were tuneful was very apparent, at practices during the week, and on the Sabbath morning calling folks to church. Their age added to their tone provided this essentially English music in a peaceful country setting.

As by ancient custom a bell at Middleton was rung at eight o'clock every Sunday morning to signify the day, whether there was an early service or no; and it was a bell, presumably the same bell, that started off the gleaners and told them when to stop.

Then, of course, the bell bore sad tidings as well as glad,

for its mournful note told of departings. Again by ancient custom, in grandfather's village it was tolled whilst the person was dying, and not when dead, since it was believed that evil spirits cannot abide the sound of a bell:

> To spede a parting soule is given to me.
> Be trimmed thy lamps as if I tolled for thee!

After the bell had fallen, and after a short pause, it was three times three for a male, three times two for a female, old or young.

Only recently, and sad to relate, when the old leaded spire was being repaired, the thatched roof of this ancient church was destroyed by fire; and by this loss a tower sanctus bell window has been disclosed, which before was obscured by a plaster ceiling.

Although grandfather was not a bell-ringer, being a Methodist, he loved his church. After all he was married there, and in that old Suffolk font, inscribed as it is in black letters with the distich 'Cryst mote us spede And helpe all at nede,' his children were baptised. Again he was on friendly terms with the rector, for it must be recalled that in those early days Methodists attended the church services in the morning. That is why their own services were often held in the afternoon, as is the case with Middleton chapel today.

Next came the Company of Singers, the parts well supplied by the miller, builder, farmer and shoemaker. They were led by an amateur orchestra, featuring the serpent, bassoon, hautboy, clarinet, flute and fiddle, and were housed in the gallery at the west end of the church. In some instances the instruments included the shawm, which was the ancestor of the modern oboe, and was often used by the bass singer as a vamping instrument.

In grandfather's church the singing was led by an old barrel organ, which I think was installed about 1864, when the interior of the church was swept of its mediaeval furnishings and mass-produced stuff significant of the Great Exhibition installed. In all probability the old orchestra went, and Tate and Brady came in by rote. As grandfather joined the village band in later years, playing the trumpet, I fear he must have envied the old windjammers in that old gallery; he loved low notes and was always seeking to get down to that bottom C. He undoubtedly would remember the players, each wearing his best Sunday smock, and each doing his very best, judging by the expressions on swollen cheeks.

That the serpent was held in high esteem, and since it is somewhat romantic in shape, one from the village church of Battisford is preserved in Christchurch Mansion, Ipswich, and another in a glass case in the church at Barking, which was played by Thomas Emsden in the church orchestra about 1830, and presented to the church by his grandchildren.

There remains the classic story of an old barrel organ refusing to stop, and having to be carried outside to continue its revolutions. However, the barrel organ at Middleton remained *in situ* until discarded sometime in the 'twenties.

But it was in the work of the fields that these Companies were most apparent. The Company of Sheep Shearers visited the farms in May or June, with their captain at their head, and they would clip two score of sheep a day, the usual price being 5s. a score, and the average clip was estimated at three and a half pounds per ewe. This occasion was as much a festival as any other, although it was closely related to sheep washings.

> Wife make us a dinner, spare flesh, neither corn,
> Make wafers and cakes, for our sheep must be shorn.

First, the barn doors would be lifted off their hinges and

made into a platform on which the shearers could work. Then at meal times the platform would be cleared, and all, including women and children, would sit round to a meal of pork, dumplings, spring cabbage and new potatoes. It is not difficult to realise how much this was enjoyed, or looked forward to. The potatoes would have been set on Good Friday, the traditional day for planting, and a pig killed in anticipation with the usual rejoicing and distribution of joints. Great pride was evinced in the shearing, done by hand, which was nothing less than an exhibition of fine art, carried out not with an eye to speed, but as something of which to be proud.

It might be recalled that a number of Suffolk flocks dated back to 1810, and were the result of a cross between a Norfolk horned ewe and a Southdown ram. The rams were put to the ewes in October, and they were fed on coleseed clover, layers and turnips. During the winter they got turnips and half a pound of rape cake each daily, and at lambing time a quarter-of-a-pound of bran as well. The flocks varied from 200 to 500 in number. A class of these was included in the Suffolk Agricultural Association's meetings in 1859, and a Suffolk Sheep Society was established in 1886. A note of some of the old official catalogues is not without interest: 'All sheep exhibited for any Prizes must have been Shorn Bare on or after 1st April in the year of the Meeting, and the date of such Shearing must form part of the Certificate of Entry.' This reminds us that a sheep is a lamb for the first year, a tegg for the second, a thieve for the third, and after that an ewe. Again, a one-shear was between two and three years old, likewise the same by a two and three-shear; and a sheepfold was known as a pinfold, while the heavy pointed iron that shone with use was a fold-pritch. This was used to make holes in the ground to receive the toes of the hurdles. (From Anglo-Saxon priccan, pungere.) Age was denoted by ear-clipping for the first two years, after that by the teeth which began to break. In some county museums the old ear-clipping books can be seen, companion pieces to those for swan marks. This form was not resorted to in Suffolk, since marking on the sheep's haunches was preferred.

Sheep-walks abounded in those days, great verdant expanses, especially in the 'sandlings' near the coast, and there were shepherds to nearly every farm. One farmer living at historic Westwood Lodge, Blythburgh, had his own sheep sales, and was widely renowned for the quality of his flocks. We can realise the value set upon a sheep even in grandfather's day, for transportation for sheep-stealing only ceased in 1868.

In the countryside of my grandfather there are certain curiously moated circular pieces of pasture, usually near an old inn. They are known as mardles, which word has more than one meaning, viz. a pond and to gossip. It is almost certain these enclosures were used by the old drovers as resting-places for their charges for the night. Drovers from Wales used to travel as far east as these parts, and would pen their sheep in hundreds (five score). The sheep would have been cleated, i.e. shod with little iron shoes (like the geese), made into the shape of their hooves and fastened over them by the blacksmith, who threw them (like the oxen) for the purpose. This was done when the sheep left the green lanes for the roads. And this was how they were counted,

> 'You a' yar [your] partner;
> Yar partner an' you!'

Haymaking or Haysel, when the Company of Harvesters first began their work, would last about three weeks. This began when the crowfoot faded to a milky white and shed its petals; when the lady's-smock and the ragged robin withered, and the sorrel turned to a brown shade. The work was often done early when the dew was still upon the grass, and then left for a day. Next the haymakers turned over the swathes and when they stopped for refreshment they hung their wooden rakes on the hedge, and stuck their shiny forks into the ground. Two days were sufficient to dry the crop, which was then carted, the pitchers sticking their steel forks into the tall cocks and handing up great sheaves to the man on the wagon. Haycarting ended in hayhome which was a tea at 5.30, and not a supper as on the other occasions. Any and everyone who had helped was invited to this, yet one other merry occasion on the farm. This work was often done by a travelling band of Irishmen who moved about from place to place finishing their cutting tasks in time to return home for their own potato harvest.

The climax of the year in farming was the Harvest or Horkey. It was then the Company of Harvesters came into their own, but instead of a captain they had a lord, and his second in command was a lady; which suggests a very early origin.

Since the work was accomplished with the scythe, the sharpening of this instrument was of paramount importance. Some men could do this well but others indifferently, thus adding materially to their labour. The usual custom was by whetstone, but in the West of England it was by a wooden strickle and riff. This latter was used with a grease horn, sand horn and a leather pad. The grease was smeared over the pad, then the sand sprinkled on this, and the strickle rubbed in the mixture and used like a whetstone. One member of grandfather's company had travelled into the 'sheres,' and spent a few harvests with a relation. Not feeling at home in such a foreign country, he returned to Suffolk, and was very voluble about these outlandish methods.

The agreement for the work would be drawn up in true legal fashion, with Earnest Money given and taken, which was as binding as the Queen's shilling in another sphere. If this was spent at the inn it was known as 'wetting the sickle!'

First would come the golden oats, then the brown ripe wheat, followed by the flaxen barley and the rich and ruddy sweep of the fields of clover, the ruby red of the trifolium, with perhaps a few pale acres of buckwheat and the yellow of rape.

The strength called forth by this constant bodily exercise from dawn to dusk, could only be sustained by repeated draughts of the home-brew. A significant utensil to be found in the shade of the 'holl' was the ranter. This is described by Forby as 'a tin or copper can in which beer is brought from the cellar and poured out into drinking vessels.' It is interesting to note the relationship between the usage of the word and its application to a certain type of preaching and speaking, sometimes experienced in grandfather's own chapel. But ranter serves as both noun and verb, and is further described as 'to pour liquor from a larger into smaller vessels.' In drinking the men would never drain the cup, but cast a little on the ground, which may have been a survival of the ancient custom of pouring out a libation to the gods.

There were, of course, various customs attending the last load from the harvest field, which might be quite a small load. It was often decked with a green bough of oak, known as the 'horkey' bough, and with flowers, sometimes with a ribbon. Or the last sheaf was decked with a bough and placed on top of the load with the prettiest girl harvester seated beside it. In East Anglia too, a green bough was always put up at the gable end of the house barn, and remained there until displaced by another at the next harvest.

It was at this time the Corn Maidens or Dollies were woven, from the last sheaf of corn reaped, and hung up in the farm-house kitchen until next harvest.

The horse teams used in these operations look picturesque enough as we see them in old photographs, but they were prone to attack by the ever scourging flies. (Incidentally, the dragon-fly was a 'hoss-needle,' of which most of the children and some of the men were 'whooly scared.') The carters would take considerable care to protect them as much as possible, fitting them with sun-bonnets, ear-pieces often gaily coloured and worked in wool, and loin nets. They even went so far in the case of a donkey (Jerusalem Pony) as to encase its legs, fore and aft, in flannel drawers, which brings to mind the old saying that an ass with golden furniture makes a better figure than a horse with a pack-saddle.

Lastly, amongst these village Companies was that of the Quoit Players, with their headquarters at the inn. They exercised themselves against rival Companies, carrying off trophies, and generally maintaining the reputation of the village. The pleasant chink of their irons and dull thud could be heard under the trees on village fête days, of which the Parson's Midder (Meadow) was the venue for that kind of thing at Middleton.

Quoit playing was essentially a country game, played here since the fifteenth century. It was thought to have derived from discus throwing, but, alas! it disappeared with the horse. It is mentioned by Shakespeare, who uses it as a verb when he makes Falstaff tell Bardolph to quoit Pistol downstairs 'like a shove-groat shilling.' Strutt in his *Sports and Pastimes* describes it as very much enjoyed by rustics, and favoured chiefly by farriers and men working with horses, for when no quoit could be found a horse-shoe was often used. Indeed, the quoit was sometimes called a shoe.

The quoit is a flattish ring of iron with an external diameter of between $8\frac{1}{4}$ inches and $9\frac{1}{2}$ inches, and an inch or two broad. It is convex on top and slightly concave underneath, the downward curving outer edge being sharp enough to cut into the soft ground. It varies in weight from 2 lb. to more than 6 lb., and rings like a bell.

Two iron pins, known as hobs, were set up 18 yards apart, and driven into the ground until only about an inch projected. Each hob formed the centre of an area about 3 feet in diameter, called an end. Ringing the pin or hob scored two points, while the quoit nearest at the end of play, scored one point. Each player had two quoits and the game was for twenty-one up.

Great skill was exercised in the throwing, and a specially skilled player could throw in such a manner as to knock off his opponent's quoit from the hob and replace it with his own. The ends would be carefully prepared with damp clay, and covered over when not in use to preserve their condition.

The tale is told of Jakey Rous, a rare old quoit player who essayed to bowl at cricket. He took careful and deliberate aim as with a quoit, tossing the ball. It would certainly have removed the middle stump, but for the batsman, who hit it for six. He was dismayed, and after an over declared that cricket had a secret beyond his skill as a quoit player.

Whilst on the subject of sport, it is interesting to note that the bat-willow tree was first discovered by Mr. James Crowe, F.L.S. (1750–1807), a surgeon of Norwich. He found the female plant wild in Suffolk and propagated it for several years in his saliscetum at Norwich.

COUNTRY CHARACTERS

Scene—An osier bed in the county of Suffolk: Keeper of beat from field above to one of his beaters on the other side of the osiers:

'Ha' yow sin Bob?'

BEATER: 'I cain't hare what yow sa'.'

KEEPER (louder): 'Ha' yow sin Bob?'

BEATER: 'I cain't hare what yow sa'.'

KEEPER (still louder): 'Ha' yow sin Bob?'

BEATER: 'Noo, ha' yow?'

Edward M. Henniker, *Eastern Counties Magazine*

◇-◇

GRANDFATHER'S friends, apart from his own kith and kin, were those of his own countryside, the genuine Suffolk argil, and included a fine collection of characters. Eccentricity was more apparent in those years than now, and was not confined to scarecrow squires, or absent-minded parsons. Individuality was the order of the day, each man and woman leading his or her life, and not necessarily conforming in pattern to their neighbours. After all, there was room for this expression of character, and if life was placid and uneventful it was often spicy, for everyone was as God made him, and oftentimes a great deal worse. Neither was the poorest among them afraid of their betters, but would give as good, or better, than they got. When, for instance, Stepper Rouse (so named because he knew to a nicety how many steps distant any given point in the village was to the pub), an inveterate poacher, was caught (a by no means rare occurrence), he openly declared to the squire that it was the grandest sport out. A reason for this apparent insolence may have been found in their names, for some bore those that were also to be found in great houses and of this they were very conscious. Sometimes at night, gathered round the fire as a clan, they would mardle about their origins, with innuendoes descending from their grandfathers (they couldn't go much further back than that), as to the reason why. Grandfather's name smacked of gentility, and appears in the pedigrees of the adjoining parish of Yoxford, collected by Elisha Davey, a local historian. He unconsciously felt it was something of which to be proud.

Poaching was in full swing in those days of large estates, and in game preserves of which Sudbourne was the peer. Although grandfather never indulged in any organised raids 'On a shiny night at the season of the year,' yet he most certainly did a little when it came to a question of a few game eggs, an occasional rabbit, hare or partridge, since his taste in those matters was nearly as good as the squire's.

There were two kinds of poachers in the district, the one of louts and ne'er-do-wells who would stick at nothing, and the quiet, almost inoffensive variety who looked upon it as a vocation, and enjoyed it as a sport to the full. In fact, if it should be that such a one got caught and a fine inflicted, it was a well-known fact that the squire would find an excuse to call at his cottage very soon afterwards with words of severe admonition on his lips and the amount of the fine in his pocket which he himself had imposed.

Such a type was poor old James Elmey, the stone-breaker, who took as much interest in Mr. Doughty's estate as he did himself, would close a gate behind him when following his moonlit craft, repair a broken hedge, or drive a stray animal into its right pasture. But his ability to knock down a cock pheasant noiselessly, swiftly, and without a trace was as great in its way as Mr. Shakespeare's in writing a sonnet. In both cases it was a matter of polished ease. Incidentally, birds (pronounced *buds*) to him were partridges, and of no other species.

Elmey was gifted with a pair of the most percipient eyes in the parish, trained by long years of work in subdued lights. He lived in a little lowly cot near the 'Bell,' called a croker, which was a study in sepia, since dwelling, table,

A performing bear (1869)

Harvest men at Poplar Farm in the Snape area. Note the frail baskets and beer jars

Shooting party with gamekeepers and brushers, East Suffolk. Note the fine spread of roof

chairs, bed, clothing, curtains were all of one colour derived from the encrusted dust and dirt of ages. Grandfather liked poor old Jimmy, whom he thought a gentleman in more ways than one, since he was not so much concerned at the price he might get for his illicit wares, for if he could pass on a meal or so to someone bedfast, or in need, he delighted in so doing. His dirty, hairy old face always bore a grin, as though life were one long joke, and he would remark, 'Mornin', Mister Barham! Do you kinder know if old Polly Wincent hev got anything for her pot? I hear as how she's ailin'!'

When not poaching or in prison he broke stones by the wayside (wages one shilling per day); a skilled occupation which he always declared he had learnt whilst in prison. (I have his wire goggles and his hammer.) Alas! it was usually the last job before the workhouse, a place with nothing but dread for these old people, but it might last for years. A perfectly innocent-looking old man, cracking *stoons* was to him second nature though primary in calling. From the character of this daytime occupation as from that at night he suffered greatly from ague, that plague of a countryman's constitution, but he had a cure for it, or at least a palliative. In his grey garden that matched his home grew a bed of groundsel, at least it grew itself since it needed no cultivation,

'Storm or wind, sun or shower,
　　still you find groundsel in flower.'

and with this he dosed himself into some relief. Moreover, he always averred that made into a poultice it was sovereign for sprains, and plucked early and tied on a bee sting would cure it.

He was an old man in my grandfather's prime, so he must have been a survival from the eighteenth century, and his knowledge of country things and ways and customs was deep and wide. He knew the difference between a stoat's run and a hedgehog's, moreover he could make and fix excellent snares, 'benders' he called them, of hazel wands and brass wire. They would hang a rat by the neck.

He would wag his old tousled head in such a knowing way, 'Do you know, Mister Barham, if you want any snipe, that old bog by the brick-arch over against Eastbridge fairly 'eaves wi' 'em!' Again, 'Have you ever noticed that chicken and animals will always climb as high as they can at night. Them owd hins, for instance, the same by the hosses. I have watched them night after night getting to the *fudder* end of that meadow.' Then, in great wisdom, 'Don't you think, Mister Barham, that's always better to know the dam rather than the sire when you're after breeding?' And grandfather's thoughts would go to his own wife.

When Jimmy got past work and was bedfast, grandfather would go and see him and mardle about old harvests and old winters. 'Ah, Mister Barham,' Jimmy would say in his philosophical way, 'that say in the old Book as how the time will come when the grasshopper shall be a burden. That's a funny old thing, they don't fare to weigh much, but that's wonderful true, for that hev come to me. Yes, that have come at last!'

Another of grandfather's friends was the Parish Clerk, whose name was Pepper, pronounced 'Pupper.' Perhaps he was not so much a friend as an acquaintance, as his habits and way of life were not those of grandfather's home.

His duties in the church included conducting Mr. White to the pulpit and fastening him in, but not to conduct him out, since the exit was left to the clergyman's own initiative. On one occasion Pepper indulged in a new pair of corduroy trousers. In those days this material was apt to smell, and these were no exception. Presently Mr. White could stand it no longer, although he was a long suffering, gentle sort of man. 'Why, Pepper,' said he, 'do you come to church in such stinking trousers?' Pepper for his part looked not so much offended as hurt. 'Why, master, they're brand-fire new; yes, yes, they're brand-fire new!' Such an expression was used by Shakespeare, and was not lost on Mr. White. He knew it signified something as new as a horse-shoe when it leaves the smithy fire, so he had to endure it.

Sometimes, of course, a visiting preacher came, and these varied in manner and methods considerably. Pepper had been known to be at his wits' end as to how to deal with some of them, others he could twizzle round his finger. An old bishop friend of the rector's almost made Pepper shake in his corduroys, and that took some doing. One Sunday morning the bishop was to preach, but for some unaccountable reason was late. Mr. White had to begin the service, when presently His Lordship arrived, complaining to himself in audible tones of his own lateness. Pepper went to conduct him to the sanctuary when he found himself being prodded in the back and told to—'Get on! Get on!' Pepper was certainly not used to that. Then, arrived in that funny little Jacobean box which was the pulpit, the bishop proceeded to wrap himself round and round in a rug or blanket as he felt the cold in his feet. He then announced his text, which was 'All we like sheep have gone astray.' The congregation settled down to listen to something they felt they could understand. It was a good sermon, for he could preach, and one hour-glass seemed not too long. Presently, warming up, he beamed with enthusiasm as he leaned over the pulpit and declared, 'But, my brethren, there are sinners everywhere. There are sinners even amongst these dear little children [pointing to the Sunday School children in their pews], and there are a vast number of *old* sinners in front of me,' waving his arms towards the rectory pew, the farmers, and including Pepper himself in his scope. There was almost the faint suggestion of a titter.

When 'sixthly and lastly' was reached it had reference to

avarice. This was dealt with thus: 'My brethren, there are several forms of avarice; one form has recently been brought home to me most unpleasantly. I had an archdeacon, a most excellent man. Well, would you credit it, he sold me a horse for fifty pounds—it is not worth ten! This, my brethren, I consider a most unpleasant form of avarice.'

That sermon was local gossip for some weeks, they 'whooly' liked it, especially the farm hands and the horsemen. They identified the archdeacon with one George Cady the horse dealer; the biggest rogue in the community.

Pepper came to die at last, and although he had dug many a grave in that very full churchyard, another had to dig his. Grandfather went to the funeral, and as those old cronies turned away, he ventured the remark to Broom, who was there also, that he hoped poor old 'Pupper' would have a better pair of boots in heaven than he possessed here— 'leastways, if he had need of such things.'

There was one figure in any country community, the most artful, cunning and wily of all, and he was the Horse Dealer. No one could match, let alone outwit him, anywhere in the rural circle. He was known for miles around, since his calling carried him in all directions; and if so known he also knew what horse was where, and the peculiarities and points of each. Moreover, he seemed to divine if you wanted to buy or sell, even before you had come to that conclusion yourself. In fact he was an encyclopaedia of horse knowledge, which included colts and fillies. Whether the horse dealer made the would-be purchaser cute, or vice-versa, I cannot say, but both were pretty tough, and there was a nice battle of wits. George Cady was one of those, and although he has been dead many a year, his fame lives on. He also might be numbered amongst grandfather's acquaintances rather than friends. In many respects he was like the devil, and if one would sup with him, one needed a wonderful long spoon; for he would singe one, be one never so careful.

He once came to see Reuben Noy because, by some country wireless message or other, he had heard that Reuben had lost his donkey. It used to be said that the 'hoss is a fule to the donkey,' so it is not advisable to try any old tricks on the latter's owner. This is the sort of thing that happened.

'Mornin', Reuben!'

'Mornin', George, bor!'

'I hear you have lost your dickey.'

'Yes, that I have, partner, an' that were a rare good donkey!'

'Well, there, bor, I'll sell you a pony instead. This one I have got in my cart.'

'That you certainly 'ont!' replied Reuben, hardly casting a glance at the animal.

'Oh,' says Cady, 'why?'

'I knew that there pony o' yours years ago. That belonged to old Flashy Free, before that belonged to you. He used to keep that on the marshes about here, and when that got down, as that had a funny habit of doing, that took a rare lot of heavy folks to get that up again. And folks about here are all wonderful thin!'

'Well, Reuben, bor,' continued Cady, in no way disconcerted, 'I have got a black pony at home. Get you into my little old cart an' I'll drive you over, and if you don't buy I'll bring you part of the way back again. What do you say to that, partner?'

'No, I say you 'ont,' concluded Reuben, and Cady knew that was the answer.

Besides being a horse-dealer, Cady was also a local preacher of the ranter type, which the Primitive Methodists were then called, and a wonderful good preacher at that, although the two callings were hardly compatible. When dealing and driving about in his sulky, with its spindle sides and tin name plate near the shafts, he was attired in customary country clothes of clay-coloured fustian, with a drab trilby cocked hat, cord trousers clasped to his legs by means of buskins, and hob-nailed boots on his feet that rang on the iron step as he jumped in and out of the trap. But on Sundays it was a different matter, and the Jekyll and Hyde nature of his character was expressed in an alpaca frock-coat with ample tails, a shovel hat, and a large gilt-edged Bible that he clasped to his bosom in a most disarming manner. If so be that anyone had courage enough amongst his listeners to accuse him of hypocrisy he would draw himself up to the full measure of his frock coat, put on an air of injured innocence and remark: 'Dear me! What a funny man you are!' This occurred once, when he was in low water financially, and took as his text 'Owe no man anything!' It was more than the listener could stand.

Naturally in dealing with horses he knew all about them, particularly how to gloss over any failings and evil traits in their character. He could 'set the wind' of a spavined mare in a most surgical manner, usually by the aid of a dose of shot, but the cure was not exactly lasting, as one might discover after the effects had worn off. However, it was a ticklish operation and called forth a good deal of admiration from those who had been 'had.'

There was no end to his tricks and stratagems, he seemed capable of inventing a new one for each occasion. For instance, he was wont to frequent the 'White Hart' at Blythburgh, which he would use as a half-way house. On one such occasion he drew up in the yard, this time accompanied by a boy. He stepped out leaving the boy to tie up the horse, while he paced up and down outside in the road, as though pondering a new sermon. Presently the womenfolk in the inn heard sundry whacks and being curious as country folks sometimes are, looked out to see what was the cause of the commotion. And there, to their astonishment, was that boy belabouring Cady's horse for all he was worth. Out rushed the girl, Rosie, with 'You naughty boy, you! What are you a doin' on? I'll go and tell Mr. Cady of you!'

The boy looked a bit crestfallen but went on with the thrashing so Rosie went in search of Cady. There he was pacing up and down as though nothing was amiss.

'Mr. Cady!' implored she, 'come you and see what your boy is a doing!'

Cady appeared to be quite alarmed and turned hot-foot at the call. He rated the boy soundly, told him he was a regular cruel-hearted lad and wouldn't go to heaven when he died. He continued: 'You're not fit to go near a hoss, and if you're not careful I'll put my whip across your shoulders, you nasty little warmint you.' But Cady soon found it convenient to pursue his vigil.

Presently, as the women kept their eyes on that nasty little muck of a boy, as also on his master, they saw Ephraim Price, the pig dealer from Blyford, drive up in his little pony cart. The two men met, exchanged the seal of the day, and began talking. After a while they noticed Ephraim unharness his pony.

'Why,' said Rosie to her mother, 'I reckon they're having a deal.'

'Well, that looks like it,' was the mother's rejoinder.

As Ephraim got his pony out of the shafts they noticed that Cady was doing the same by his, and soon the ponies had exchanged shafts. With that they parted, each to his home.

Some weeks later, Ephraim was again at the 'White Hart.' As he lingered over his pint mug Rosie, ever curious, asked him how he had got on with the pony he had exchanged with Cady.

'That blarmed pony,' growled Ephraim, 'that's the laziest hoss I've ever set eyes on. Do you know the last time I went to Saxmundham market, that took six hours to get home. I couldn't get it along nohow!'

'Oh,' continued Rosie, 'perhaps that was why Cady's boy was a setting in to that, just before you came along. We couldn't make that out at the time.'

'What!' exclaimed the nettled Ephraim, 'was that his old trick? I wish I had known that then. But there, I might have known Cady would have been up to something.'

It was the same when Cady went to Walberswick and bought a calf. He put it in his cart under a net and jogged along home to Yoxford, along the Blythburgh Road, past the old stone cottages and the barn which stands sentinel and lonely on the hill by Hinton. In so doing he had to pass a small-holding kept by a man named Holmes, who, of course, he knew. He stopped, and, as he expected, Holmes was at home. He put on his best Sunday manner and asked Holmes if he could do with a nice little calf? 'For I have got the prettiest little bit of a thing as ever you saw!'

'How much do you want for it?' asked Holmes, coming to the back of the cart in as disinterested a way as he could.

'Well, there,' replied Cady, 'I have bought it, but I don't fare to want to take it home. To tell you the truth, I give fifty shillings for it, and you can have it for what I give. I have only just bought it, and you can see by my books what I have give.'

Holmes thought a bit, and agreed, and paid there and then. (Cady would certainly have seen to that.) Being a careful man, and not caring to see anything going to waste, Holmes kept the calf tethered by the roadside on the grass verge, to eat its own living as it were. Some days later, who should come along but the original owner, and seeing Holmes not far distant, hailed him: 'I see you ha' got my calf there! Did you buy that off Cady?'

'Yes, yes,' replied Holmes, 'And if you've a mind to tell me, what did Cady give you for that?'

'Well, there, bor!' replied the farmer, 'old Cady's a funny old chap, he said he'd give me fifty shillings for un, but I were to give him twenty shillings back again. So I did!'

'Oh, did he,' ejaculated Holmes, 'he hasn't forgot how to

be artful. I give him what he give you, but he forgot to give me back the sovran!'

Cady was a rum 'un all right, and he knew how many beans made five. Even if he was a preacher and observed Sundays in the traditional manner, he couldn't keep his eyes off a bit of horseflesh. 'Friend George!' he once asked the quiet master of the 'White Hart,' 'if that wasn't Sunday, how much would you take for that little brown mare o' yours?'

'Ah,' replied George, 'I don't sell mares on Sunday, and if you want to know the price of her you must come again tomorrow!'

But Cady could take you into his confidence, say for instance that you had done a deal with him, and then asked him what was the matter with the horse you had just bought, he would as lief as not tell you, 'That have a nasty habit of turning round in the road!' As you would probably have found out for yourself in a short space of time.

Many and various were the deals he had made. Once from Norwich he brought home a brood of Shetland ponies. He managed to get them along to his yard, and when his wife saw the curious collection she wrung her hands in despair. 'What on earth shall we do with that lot?' She was sure he had bitten his fingers this time.

'Well, my dear!' remarked Cady in his best sang-froid manner, 'they're like the babes, they bring their love with them.' And so they did, for the gentry for miles around scrambled to see the little dears, and buy them for their children. It proved the best deal he had ever made.

Yes, Cady's mares, colts, calves, foals and all the other animals have passed long since to the knacker's yard, while he has gone on the wings of the flying horse to heaven. I wonder if he as he dismounted suggested to St. Peter, 'That's a rare high stepper, master! If this wasn't heaven, how much would you take for he?'

Our next friend is a woman, who was but a girl in grandfather's time, but she was of his past in her associations and memories. She was known to everyone as 'Blind Liza.' Her real name was Miss Walnut, but no one ever thought of addressing her as such.

Through her mother she was a Stollery. Now there has always been a Stollery in the village; they lived for generations after generations at Stulps, and farmed the fields. Some were sailors and went down with their ships, others filled various labouring jobs, including Liza's father, who went to work on the new railroad, in those far-off days when railways began to run almost everywhere. He travelled as far south as Three Bridges, Sussex, and was there killed on the road by which he had hoped to live.

Liza lived in a little one-roomed cottage up an alleyway between the 'housen.' She could just see, so she would sit, hour after hour, when her jobs were done, with her hands folded limply in her lap, and always her hat on her head as though expecting to be summoned out at any minute. A frail spare little body, in neatly patched ancient clothes, wearing a bodice with a high neck, held closely fastened with a large round brooch in which was a lock of hair; and a row of small spheroid buttons that ran, guardsman-like, from neck to bodice band. A tight little mouth, and a pair of almost sightless eyes that flickered under long lashes. She would sit there, statuesque and impotent, quietly reflecting.

When you entered, she took not the slightest notice, as though unconscious of your presence, and yet answered your first question or greeting as though you had been there all the time. She lived not quite alone, for she had three cats—a she who stayed at home, a he who went out at night, and a kitten.

'How are the cats a-doing?' you might ask.

'Oh, they're all right, thankee,' she would reply. 'But the old Tom will go out abroad, so I don't fare to think I shall have him long. Someone told me as they saw him down the "maashes." "Oh," I say, "well there, I can't follow that about." When he come home yesterday I say, "How you do smell o' rabbits, bor!" You can't keep them out o' traps when they once go a rabbitin'. '

Clocks ticked all about the one tiny room, for she was passionately fond of them, and knew if they were fast or slow, yet none were striking clocks. A loud tick of American origin had belonged to her granny, but the others were of her own choice and acquisition. One, however, she lacked, and that was a grandfather. She had always meant to have such but it had not come her way. Once or twice she had gone to an auction but always someone had out-bid her and she was too poor to pursue, so she had to let it go with that resigned attitude which was her life.

In the muddle that was her home, just under the lattice window, stood a nice little piece, an old chestnut hutch, and on this rested some of her geraniums. It was nicely polished on turned shiny legs, with a stretcher rail running round the four sides. An old dealer, ever on the look out for treasures hid in cottages, had coveted this and been rash enough to offer her ten shillings for it. But if she was blind she wasn't silly, and although that was a large sum of money to her, she decided it was worth more than that. Besides she kept her food in it, or at least the part that was surplus. Then, again, it was a nice bit of furniture that just suited her one crowded window, and she would have been lonely without it for it had belonged to her grandmother, and to quite a respectable line of Stollerys.

She had not always lived in this one-roomed hovel, which was somehow carved out of an old cottage, for the next door neighbour had a room above it, but in a little house at the end of the passage way, until that had fallen about her ears. Gradually, piece by piece, it had gone into ruin for the lack of timely aid, and one night in a gale (she called it a tempest) the gable-end went and left poor Liza in bed in a room with only three sides. 'Lawks!' if she had known that was going to happen she wouldn't have undressed, or gone to bed. It woke her up into a regular frap, and she got dressed as well and as quick as she could, made her way off the tottering floor, down the fragile stairs and out through the wreckage into the haven of a friend's cottage. 'That's just like them old landlords, they 'on't do a thing until they're regular forced to—and not then! Sooner see the places fall down and scare folks. Come to think on it, I reckon the old place had only held together with years and years of paper that folks kept a sticking on top of one another. Regular filled up the crevices between the old wooden posts. But there, it gave way at last and let in the cold wind. That was a wonder I hadn't caught my death of cold.'

When the squire came to see her, as he often did, when passing through the village on his chestnut, she would hop up right quick, give him a royal curtsy and dust a chair for him to sit himself down. 'Set you down, master, set you down!'

'Your geraniums are coming on well, Liza!' he might say.

'Yes, sir, they do. I broke that bit off yesterday, so I stuck that in that little old pot; but there, I think that's a doing!'

'They smell nice too, Liza, especially the oak one.'

'Do you think so, now, sir? Well there, my old grand-mother couldn't abear that. "You have been a stirrin' that old plant again, Liza," she'd say. "I can't stand that nohow, that fare real horrid!" '

'Is there anything you want, Liza?' he'd ask discreetly.

'No thankee,' she'd say. 'I fare to manage nicely. Folks about here are wonderful kind. I don't fare to lack nothing.'

'Have you got plenty of candles and kindling, Liza?'

'Yes, thankee kindly, sir. I always keep a good fairing of them in case I want a light in the night. I always think of what my old grandmother used to say: "Get the tinder box a ready for the mornin', Liza gal, an' keep the lint an' brimstone dry, else you'll repent on't." '

When the squire rose to go, and made as though he would put back his chair to the wall, she'd be too quick for him. 'Don't you do that, sir, don't you do that! That's a sign as you won't come here no more; an' I hope you'll be so good as to come again when you're passing. You have been some good to me, that you have!' A curtsy would speed his passing.

'Good-bye, Liza!' he would say as he stooped to pass out of her doorway, 'and if ever I have the misfortune to lose my sight—which God forbid—I hope I'll be as cheerful about it as you. Don't fail to let me know if you want anything.' And before going, with a deft movement he would place a little gold piece under the nearest geranium pot. And she would know where to find it.

On the chimney breast was an old photograph, taken on glass by a travelling photographer. It was of a country beauty in close-fitting bonnet and wide flouncing clothes in which some silk appears, complete with curls set about a Romany face of loveliness. That was her mother. Not far removed was another, less attractive portrait of an old woman in her late eighties, with mouth open and her head set askew on her neck as though it remained in place with difficulty. So many years it had thought and planned but now any moment it might fall back, dead! That was her grandmother, known as 'Shakey-head Stollery'; of whom the children were 'whooly' afraid.

Indeed, grandmother had brought her up. Liza's mother had died, or disappeared when she was a babe, and had figured so little in her life that Liza seemed to have slipped a generation. One heard little or nothing of father or mother, but a great deal of grandmother, and she belonged to the past of hard severity, privation, poverty. Not the good old days of fabled history, but the starkness of reality, expressed in labour, frost, snow, burning sun or keen winds. Sometimes the thoughts of grandmother were not rose-tinged, but of a rather cantankerous old woman who had passed through the mill of life. Grandmother was a 'rum old gal who didn't like to see people enjoying themselves over much.' She didn't like music, or church bells, or her own times, and too often thought things were all of a jamble; or in her own words: 'An' I don't fear snow, nor cold, nor sickness, nor death; for I am not one o' they as is so desperately fond o' life!'

Liza's grandmother was a chapel woman and was a very regular attendant until she and another woman fell out with them over a tea-meeting. It appears they had paid for a tea two years running and never got one, so she declared she'd never go inside the place again and later on when she might have changed her mind, she *dussent*. She went to Aldringham chapel for a long while, some folks used to call for her and take her there in their pony cart, but they moved away and then she walked the seven miles until she couldn't go any more. She would lie down on the stone heaps by the roadside, she was so tired. And then she didn't go anywhere for a long time. Mr. White came to see her with an invitation to the old village shrine.

'No,' she would say, 'I 'on't come to that cold old place!'

'Well,' said he, ignoring the ungracious refusal, 'I have come to tell you there's a church in the village, and that isn't far away. I'd like you to know that. Perhaps that's not served up on the same dish, but it's the same meat.'

She thought it over a bit and then relented, so she became a regular attendant there, but her earlier love was strong. She would say to Liza, 'I want you to carry me to Aldringham when I go!'

'Oh,' Liza would reply, 'you know there won't be no money to do that!' But she persisted and it worried poor Liza. 'Why can't you be satisfied to lie here?' she would ask. 'Grandfather lay here, why do you want to go to Aldringham?' Two or three years before the end she gave up the thought. 'I don't know what I should have done if she had persisted!' Then Liza would ruminate:

'Yes, that old geranium was poor old grandmother's, an' when she died that wouldn't fare to thrive nohow. Well, they do say "tie a bit o' black on that, an' that'll do!" so I did, an' after a bit that got on better. She used to say to me, "Pity, gal, you worn't born a day sooner, an' then you'd a bin born on Trinity Fair." She was full o' them funny old sayings as never was! Perhaps you know, them old fairs were thought a deal on by folks them days. There was Trinity Fair at Southwold, and Colfer [Cold Fair]. Why, the landlord o' the "Crown" at Westleton used to give his customers hot elderberry wine the night afore Colfer.' (December 9th or 21st.)

'Grandmother used to go to Trinity Fair the night before to see them all a coming in. They looked a rum old lot, especially the women wi' their naked legs, and their hair all done in curls. A lot of folks about here used to do that, and garp at their old wagons an' things.

'Sometimes we'd all go—walk there, o' course. I used to regular like that. I could see better then; an' that was all so different from this quiet old place. Old women a dancin', folks playin' the fiddle, and everyone as jolly as could be. But there, one o' the things I remember most was havin' a penny to spend. I didn't get many o' they, I can tell you. I see a pair o' blue beads [a necklace] and that was a penny but grandmother say: "No gal, you can't have it, you buy a bun instead; that'll do you more good!" An' I wur so fond o' them beads!

'Yes, grandmother 'ud tell her mind right quick. Sometimes she'd fare to shout the house down, an' grandfather 'ud say, "Don't you shout so, an' take on like that!" But there, she had to work some hard. At one time she used to go to Sandy Lane Farm at Dunwich. Have to get there before eight o'clock, an' work in the field, hoein', or pullin' beet, or whatever there was to do, an' they didn't leave off afore five o'clock. And all she got wur a shillin' a day. If she got the chance, she'd go a bakin', or brewin', even candle-making to earn a few coppers. Poor old gal, let's hope she's at rest now!

'Grandfather died when he was only sixty. He fell ill, and fared as though he'd like to see Doctor Balls from Hales-worth. So he sent for him an' he come along.

' "Ah," he say, "I suppose you want me to tell you the truth?"

' "Yes," say grandfather, "that's what I sent for you for."

' "Well," he say, "you have got the same complaint as I have, an' I know where mine is a going to take me. I'll give you some medicine, but I can't do any more for you than Bailey can." And the next week when Bailey come he give the same sort o' medicine as Balls, so we knew he knew what wur wrong wi' grandfather. Later on when he got worse he say to grandmother: "Go you an' look in my box, an' see how much money I ha' got there." So she did, she counted it out an' say: "There's five pound here!"

' "Is that all gal? I thought there wur more'n that!"

' "No," she say, "there ain't, an' I hain't had on't."

' "Oh," he say, "well that'll do to put me under the ground, an' you'll have to manage as best you can."

' "Well, there," she say, "I suppose that's what you a married me for!"

'He say, "That's how that have turned out, but there's my watch, but I don't want you to part with that, 'cept for bread!" And she never did.

'I have got the old watch now, and some time ago I had that on the mantelshelf, an' an old dealer—a regular hand-to-mouth liar—come along here a selling spectacles. He regular crazed me until I bought a pair. I told him—"I'm blind! I don't want them old glasses!" but I bought a pair to get rid o' him. They come in handy sometimes when one o' the neighbours come in to read or write a letter, an' they can't fare to see me, or they've left their sights at home. He see my old watch a lying there—"I'll buy that orf o' you!" he say. "I'll give you half a crown for that!"

'"No, you certainly 'on't," I say.

'"Well, that arn't any good, that's only fit for boiling up," he say.

'"So that may be," I say, "but you 'on't have it! That belonged to grandfather, an' I 'on't part wi' it."

'An' so he went on, but I wouldn't listen to him, an' when he'd gone I put that away in my old chest, an' that's there now!

'Oh, I fare to hickle along good tidy. I don't go to church alone, but then someone always calls for me, an' I enjoy the service right well. I can't hear all the preacher say, but that don't matter a lot. They ain't the kind we used to have when I was a girl; they were thought a deal on then. Take poor old Isaacson at Westleton, he was some nice old fellow, wi' a great old white beard. When Woods the farmer started a workin' on Good Friday, a ploughin' an' such-like, he had an accident. He didn't think anything about coming to church, or that sort of thing, an' the pole o' the cart stuck in the horse's chest; an' that died.

'When Isaacson heard that he went off to see Woods, an' he say: "That were a judgement on you! God in heaven can see you wherever you go; that's no use a hiding! He can see you!" That regular turned Woods right round, an' he wouldn't have none o' his men work on a Good Friday after that, an' he come to the church wonderful regular.'

So Liza sat by her fireside, summer and winter since there was always a fire in the grate, and reflected on the days of her grandmother, on the happenings in the village, beyond the confines of which she did not wish to venture—

> Day unto day:
> Still ending and beginning still.

THE SQUIRE AND HIS RELATIONS

'The ancientest house, and the best for housekeeping in this county or the next, and though the master of it write but squire, I know no lord like him.'

Merry Beggars

<><><><><><><><><><><><><><><><><><><><><><><><><><><><><>

THE Squire was a cultured man of a cultured family with many quarterings. He lived in a large house set deep in a very beautiful park, yet not too deep that it could not be seen in glimpses from the road, and some portion of its western aspect by reason of a footpath that skirted a ha-ha which marked the limit of its lawn. The house or hall, built in the early part of the eighteenth century, was added to, embellished by a ballroom and picture gallery, together with outbuildings and water tower, to the certain impoverishment of its owners. But it had no bathroom. There were, of course, the usual plethora of servants—housekeeper, cook, kitchen-maid, butler, footman, coachman, valet, upper and under house-maids, maid-of-all-work, laundry maid, etc. etc. etc.

These may have compensated for the poor sanitary arrangements and made life possible, for the former involved a huge cesspit, which was a herculean task to empty. This was done at midnight when the moon was at the full with all the windows securely fastened and a bottle of gin for the sanitary squad.

The regnant squire when my grandfather was very young was a Squarson—the Rev. Charles Montagu Doughty, who married Frederica Beaumont, daughter of the Honourable and Rev. Frederick Hotham, Rector of Dennington and Prebendary of Rochester. By several astute marriages the Doughtys had added wide lands to their estates, part of which was at Martlesham, acquired by marrying the heiress of the Goodwins of Martlesham Hall. This Doughty also was a Squarson.

146

THE SQUIRE AND HIS RELATIONS

The Rev. Charles Montagu Doughty had two sons, the elder being Henry Montagu and the younger Charles Montagu. Henry must have been quite young when he succeeded to the paternal estates. His son in turn, Lieutenant-Colonel Charles Doughty-Wylie, gained a posthumous V.C., leading the last desperate charge from the Horse-of-Troy at Gallipoli, while his brother commanded one of the last built great Dreadnoughts in the main Fleet at that time.

But it was Charles Montagu Doughty, second son of the Rev. Charles, born on August 19, 1843, who gained undying lustre for the family.

He came into the world a sickly child, and was baptised by his father almost immediately, but he lived to undergo the severest hardships, and to carry his life in his hand.

My grandfather must have known and seen this studious youth and touched his cap to him, for he was ever about his father's fields, since he devoted himself to the study of Suffolk chalk, and flint implements from Hoxne, before going up to Caius College where his grandfather and father had been before him. He is described when an undergraduate as shy, nervous and very polite, with no sense of humour. That his Suffolk origin and beginnings coloured his life and subsequent endeavours is not surprising, and the lovely setting of his home must have been ever subconsciously colouring the conditions in which he found himself. That his home associations were strong is evinced by the fact that he presented the old schoolmaster-sexton of his ancient round-towered church, one Jesse Pipe, with a copy of his *Arabia Deserta*. That poor old Pipe (a great bell-ringer and lover of the tenor bell) didn't know what to do with it is not surprising, since some critics of his day found 'the style of the book so peculiar as to be at times hardly intelligible'; so he placed it in his side cupboard out of harm's way, to be brought out as a great possession when anyone should call who knew the family. Poor Pipe was probably dead when a later discerning public (second-hand booksellers to wit) decreed it to be worth its weight in gold.

The old Suffolk brogue comes out now and again, as in this: 'As it was night there came the waits, of young camp followers with links; who saluting every pavilion were last at the Persian's lodgings, their place, as they are strangers and schismatics, doubtless for the avoiding of strife, is appointed in the rear of all the great caravan with the refrain bes-salaamy bes salaamy, . . . go in peace, good speed, heigho the largess!' That old farming custom crept in, as also his country breeding and knowledge: 'Their clotted dates, if they have any, are stived in heavy pokes of camel hide.' And: 'In the early morning Ghroceyh milked our thelul (camel) and brought me the warm bever.'

Doughty had the eye of a poet and nothing escaped him, so that all the little details were set down with the greatest accuracy, as the Staffs were to find in the first Great War. But he himself wrote: 'When the printing and publishing of the *Arabia Deserta* volumes was completed, I found little interest was taken in such work at home. I felt therefore I had done therein what was in my power and as the Arabs say, I might wash my hands of it; and could turn now to what I considered my true life's work with the Muse.'

Doughty had indeed cause to mention this apathy, for having completed this work of some 1,150 closely packed pages, comprising 600,000 words, he offered it to several of the leading publishers in turn, who all rejected it, making the rather unkind criticism that it needed re-writing by a skilled and competent writer. Doughty's answer to this was, 'It is chaste and right English of the best time and without a word of costermongery and very hard for the best unstudied pens to amend.' After the usual round of travel his own University agreed to publish it, and although the result was a disappointment to their Press, involving a loss, yet they were glad to have launched this work which later generations were to acclaim.

From then onwards, following his beloved Chaucer and Edmund Spenser, Doughty embarked on the epic poem. First then came *Adam Cast Forth*, followed by *Dawn in Britain*, then *The Cliffs* and *The Clouds*, *The Titans*, and *Mansoul*, considered his finest poem.

And so on January 17, 1926, this tall man with a beard, once red but now grey and old, died, and was cremated at Golders Green. Amongst the few mourners there were but two men of letters to mark the occasion, one John Freeman, a minor poet of his era, and another 'unrecognised in the uniform of the R.A.F. giving the name of "Shaw".'

OLD CURES

Mrs. Smith, *loquitur*:

'Well, mum, my husband he was that sadly that I goes to the Doctor to ask 'im for some physic. He give me some pills, and said I'd better take 'em home and give 'em to my husband with speed.

'Well, yer see, we hain't got no speed, but we got an ode scuppit, and so I puts the pills in the ode scuppit [shovel], and copped 'em up and down ter went!'

◇◇

THE countryside was as full of cures as the towns were full of patent medicines. Whereas the latter found their public by means of advertising, the former were the inheritance of many generations handed on and down as closely guarded secrets in families and through persons by whom they were practised. Like the sunshine and the fragrance of the fields and hedgerows out of which they sprang, they were in the main free; while the town cures produced rich harvests for their vendors, with a portion for the State. Some village folk had a 'say' (taste) for the doctor's medicine (which came in a bottle with the label tied round the neck, not stuck on the side as now) while others looked upon it with suspicion, as being nowhere near so efficacious as their own family concoctions. Harriet Marjoram boasted she had never taken a drop of doctor's medicine all her long life. However, she was quite glad to see Bailey if he called, and was agreeable to be examined by him if needs be. When she had a bad leg he jokingly remarked to her: 'There now, Harriet, old gal, if you'll come or send to mine I'll give you a bottle of port.' 'Thet you 'on't,' was her somewhat ungracious reply; 'I'd fancy a drop a yare wine, but thet's wot you'd be a puttin' in it as wudn't be tew my likin'.'

This curative panoply was the result of a wide and deep understanding of nature, with a background of skill derived maybe from wandering members of the Church, but much of it the inheritance from a pagan ancestry and primeval worship, with charms playing a leading part. Witchcraft spells, evil-eye, and acts of a wrathful God lingered on to be placated, cast off or by-passed the best way possible. Superstitions and superstitious practices lingered on, and were more apparent in that nineteenth century, though they still exist today. It was quite common for a country doctor in Victorian times to have patients who would implore of him to 'take it off them.' One farmer's wife in the next parish to grandfather's declared she knew the woman who had 'put it on' herself and her son. When lying in bed they had heard a 'whiff! whiff! whiff!' above them, and then it was being loosed on them.

It must be remembered there was a large amount of stoicism and resignation in Victorian folk. A bowing to the inevitable disguised as the Divine Will, and a stolid endurance which amounted almost to callousness. Yet there was that heroic bearing of the burden of pain, and fearlessness in the face of overwhelming odds that has been only equalled by that noble and very select body of V.C.s. Surgery was still primitive, certainly in the middle years of the century, and the harvest field always seemed to provide a crop of casualties, often fatal. Think again of the breed of seamen in the days of sail, and the courage evinced by the lifeboatmen up and down our coast. January gales and doubtful craft took immense toll of village lads in those hard winters just as cholera, yellow fever and bloody flux decimated the ranks of the county regiments serving on foreign stations. These empire builders went out from the countryside in regiments at full strength, to return, if ever, as skeleton cadres, leaving their comrades behind under such epitaphs as:

> I'm billeted here by Death,
> And here I must remain;
> When the last trumpet sounds,
> I'll rise—and march again.

In country villages the extraction of teeth was often done by a blacksmith who kept extractors for that purpose as well as those for horses. The poor farmer's lad, fed on flick pork and dumplings with black treacle, arriving with aching jaw would be greeted by the man of iron with: 'Come yew in the travise [blacksmith's open shed], bor! an' put yare backside on this pail.' Then when the offending tooth had been lugged out with an iron grip: 'Yew fare tew look quare, bor, that yew dew! Gew yew off tew the pub an' git yareself some rum; thet'll put yew tew rights.' And it did.

The simples, administered in the form of teas and oint-ments, draughts and poultices (but if mixed and boiled for some time they were known as decoctions), were in earlier and more refined forms products of the hands of the Lady of the Manor and her still room. They then took the form of cordials, juleps, aromatic waters and medicines. It is also true to say that the British Pharmacopoeia owes much to these herbal remedies, and yet abhors the quack. Evelyn once said: 'If the medicinal prospectus of the leaves, barks, berries, etc., were thoroughly known, I cannot tell what our countrymen could ail for which he might not find a remedy from every hedge, either for sickness or wound.'

Camomile flowers, tinctured with gin, could be made into a poultice efficacious for tonsillitis and diphtheria; and the leaves of the plant, mixed with those of yarrow and agrimony, would make a herb tea. Coltsfoot *alias* foalsfoot, was good for bronchitis and asthma; but the former could be counter-acted by wearing a string (or was it a charm) of blue beads round the neck, and they were sold for this purpose in Nor-wich shops. Incidentally, Norwich also held the distinction of possessing a factory for the making of pill-boxes, in the early years of Victoria's reign. The leaves and flowers of the marsh-mallow were made into an ointment to be rubbed on boils, and a decoction of the leaves was good for a strain. A poultice was made from stewed groundsel, and one for sore legs from chickweed. On the other hand, teasel roots would cure abcesses. 'Poor Man's Friend' was a red ointment. This rather confused one countryman when he went to the Great Exhibition and saw the gentlefolk eating raspberry ices which he took to be this red ointment. How they could eat that, he didn't fare to know.

Dock leaves were good for galled feet, green broom for the kidneys, dandelion root for the liver, mistletoe for epilepsy, dwarf hyperion for heart trouble, parsley and break stone for the gravel, pennyroyal for women's complaints, rue pills for a tonic; and borage relieved depression. Then folks were counselled to 'take enough of powdered horse beans' for heartburn, and similarly of powdered acorns for diarrhoea. Cottage homes usually kept a supply of these dried for this purpose. Worms could be treated with chopped leaves of the garden box, or by wearing a raw carrot next to the heart, or taken internally first thing in the morning. Snails were a safeguard against consumption.

Parsley provided an eye-salve, and was said to be the secret of the gipsies' good eyesight. And as everyone knows, the wearing of gold ear-rings helps the sight, hence their use by old shell-backs. A stye could be dispersed by rubbing it with a gold ring; and a specific for falling sickness was to wear a ring on the little finger made from a half-crown piece taken at the Holy Table. But then, confirmation was good for rheumatism, the bishop's right hand being most efficacious.

Whooping-cough, that scourge of infancy, had a wide range of cures. One very common form was to drink the remains of a saucer of milk, of which the ferrets had taken the other part. Norfolk children suffering from this complaint were sent to meet the incoming tide, and as it ebbed so the cough went. Ringworm, on the other hand, could be cured by the sweat of an axe. For this it was necessary to make a bonfire and put green stuff on it to cause smoke rather than flame. The axe was held in the smoke and then applied to the affected part, drawing it along to leave the sweat behind. For shingles one went to the blacksmith's shop and put a handful of wheat in his iron ladle, holding it over the fire to melt out the oil. A headache could be cured by wearing a snake's avel (skin) inside one's hat, and was considered a certain cure. Sloe wine was good for the colic.

The elder tree or eldern had certain mystical charms. It was considered to be the tree from which the Cross was made, and was a safe shield in a thunderstorm, as it would not be struck by lightning. It was often planted by old dairy windows to keep the devil out of the milk, and prevent him interfering with the butter; and served as a screen for the retreat in the garden (*alias* the bumby). It was also planted near sheep pens, the leaves being bruised and rubbed on the sheep by the shepherds, as the smell kept away flies. Then too, it provided a lotion, made from the flowers and shoots, which was dabbed on the parts of a horse affected by flies. A piece stuck in the gooseberry bushes at the right time prevented the arrival of the magpie moth, and thus the gooseberry caterpillar. And in its stages there were three good things to be gained. The green buds could be turned into a tonic, the flowers into an ointment, and the fruit into an excellent wine, often used as a cordial. And dried blossoms could be brewed into a tea, useful in measles to bring out the spots. Then it also grew 'toothache twigs,' one of these shoots could be held in the mouth and then transferred hurriedly to a hole in the wall, exclaiming: 'Depart evil spirit!'

Jaundice could be cured with the juice of the barberry, or by wearing the mossy substance (robins' pincushions) which grow on the wild briar, suspended round the neck by a string long enough to reach the navel.

These cures lead us naturally to the consideration of country sickness, with my grandfather's village providing the examples. First, the stomach was known as *cogs of the wheel*, while *jot* stood for the paunch or stomach. *Pin o' the throat* was the uvula. The wind-pipe was the *stroop*, while the big toe was the *Tom toe*. *Tong* did not mean the tongue so much as the voice that comes from it: 'I ollust know yar tong'; whilst similarly *tooth* really stood for taste: 'I can't tooth thet!' *Fit* stood for feet, *huckle* for hip, and *poke* for the womb.

Confirmed was to be obstinately incurable: 'He is ill with a confirmed consumption.' *Crickle* or *cruckle* was to sink down with faintness; while a *down-pin* was a person in poor health, or out of spirits. *Dozzy* was to be giddy, bewildered: 'A fare as dozzy as a coot'; but to *dudder* was to shiver with the cold. To be *gaggy* was to be sick at the stomach; while to 'lie in' was a euphemism for groaning, but a miscarriage or premature birth was a *mishap*. *Hulkin* was a covering for a sore finger, while *bultin* was a throbbing pain; likewise *gelver* was to throb; but *mort* was to be at death's door. *No matters*, was to be in poor health: 'Ma husban' dun't fare no matters!' A squeamish eater was a *pingler*; to choke was to *quackle*: 'He quackled ta ded by bleeding from the throat.' *Rasp* was to belch; *sunket* to rear delicately; and *winders* were the women who laid out and watched a dead body; while *out* was tolling for the dead.

An *absey* was a sore or angry boil, likewise a *push*; *Anthony's Fire* was erysipelas, while *bloody flux* was the dysentery. *Black cap* was the black jaundice. *Gullet* did not describe that part of the anatomy, as one might suppose, but a swollen protuberance: 'He got a gullet under his throat,' which was probably goitre. To sprain one's self was to *jink*. To be restless or fidgety was to have the *pinhustles* or *whywiffles*. *Ret* or *wret* was a wart, while a *rove* was a congealing scratch or wound; and to be *rovy* was to be itchy, lousy, or scabby; but to be *scratchy* was to be sore: 'A scratchy throat.' Sickness was understood as *sekenesse*, and *spotted fever* described measles, scarlet and putrid fevers. *Tad* was excrement, but *tissicks* an irritating cough, or coughing spasms. To stagger was to *titter* or *teeter* (a see-saw was a *tittermatorter*); while the ring-worm was the *titty worm*. *Weer* was to be worn-looking or pale; while to whimper like a peevish child was to *whinnock*. *Ablaze* was to be full of inflammation: 'His hand is ablaze'; while *ranch* was a deep scratch. *Nettle-springe* was nettle rash, while *stiny* was a sty or inflamed eyelid, but *twidle* was a small pimple. And to end all: 'His be a tidy brunt this time, ill of a *universal* dropsy!'

Naturally they had some rough-and-ready cures, as the landlord of the 'Bell' once discovered. He had a whitlow come on his thumb; and that gave him what-for, I can tell you. He nursed the old thing and cossetted it until he didn't know what to do with himself. Stepper Rouse called, as usual, and found him in a very poor state, but hoped he'd soon get relief. The next day he called again, and naturally wanted to know how things were.

'Oh,' said George Beaton, 'that's cured, but I hain't seen the chap what cured it since thet wur done!'

'How's thet?' enquired Stepper.

'Well,' continued George, 'a chap comed in hare yisterday arternune an' say tew me. "Wud yew like me tew cure thet fur yew?"

'"Thet I shud," I say!

'"Well," he say, "I'll dew it, but yew mustn't see what I dew. Put yare owd thumb on the table bor, sew, an' look at thet picture hinder; an' yew mustn't tarn yare hid. Dew yew promise me thet?"

'"Yis," I say, "I'll promise, I shud be some glad tew git rid on't."

'And wi' thet, he brings down his owd stick on my thumb wi' sich a thwack, an' he out o' thet door afore I cud tunn round; an' I ain't sin him since. But thet cured my thumb!'

Baker Free once scratched his hand with a rusty piece of

wire, and it would not heal. As a last desperate resource, he sent his son Jethro to look for the actual strand of wire that had caused the wrong. Having found it he brought it home, and polished it bright, to help cure his father's hand.

Yes, they had their remedies, used as a cure or a prophylactic.

And their oblique compliment to the doctor might be: 'Don't you remember grandfather? Whoi, he died under you!'

COUNTRY CALENDAR

Dirty days hath September,
April, June and November,
February has twenty-nine—
I take you for my Valentine,
All the rest have thirty-one,
Without a single glimpse of Sun,
And if one month had thirty-two,
They'd all be dull and dirty too.
Edward M. Henniker.
The Eastern Counties Magazine, 1900

<hr>

THE countryman's year was in no way complete without its Calendar, which was an illuminated manuscript of red-letter days. There was of course the Sporting Calendar observed rigidly by the squire and certain farmers, which contained significant dates; and the Racing Calendar for those who could follow it. But there was also that deeper, fuller perpetual calendar, read and known by all; and it was by this that the year revolved. It started with Hallowe'en, and certain mystic fires, and found its climax either on May Day, or St. John's Eve, with other fires. This day-to-day record continued until the First World War.

Most of these anniversaries revolved around the Church's Year, although probably pagan in origin, and many had regard to the weather in prospect which is not surprising when life in the country was so dependent on local harvests. If one could read the sky faultlessly, as many of them could, one was that much in advance of one's neighbours and could as it were snatch a crop. After all, bad seasons were a national disaster. It must be borne in mind, however, that these dates were eleven days later than now, owing to the revision of the Julian Calendar. Hence in some country districts today, such as grandfather's, Michaelmas Day is still observed on the old day, October 11th.

In seventeen hundred and fifty three
The style it was changed to Popery,
But that it is liked we don't all agree;
Which nobody can deny.

When the countryfolk first heard of the Act,
That Old Father Time was condemned to be racked,
And robb'd of his style, which appears to be fact;
Which nobody can deny.

First then, reading the year from January, came New Year's Day. This was observed by bringing something into the house before anything was taken out, which was usually a little piece of split wood that had to be burnt at once:

> Here's a little piece of wood,
> And I hope it will do you good.

Boys performed this office, and it was to ensure that things should be coming into the house all the year, and not merely going out of it.

Then came Twelfth Day (January 6th) when the wren was annually hunted and killed; or caught alive and placed in a Wren House, which was a cage decorated with coloured ribbons, and taken from house to house.

Twelfth Night, which is really the Eve of old Christmas Day, when it was commonly held that the rosemary flowered at midnight and cattle turned to the east:

> On Twelfth Night, daylight increases the length of a deer's leap.

Plough Monday was that following Twelfth Day, when the labours of the plough usually began. In some districts Plough Plays and Plough Jags were performed, featuring the

Straw Man. This part was taken by a big man who was covered all over with straw, with a long tail that trailed behind him. Or he took the form of a Hobby Horse, wearing a wicker sieve round his middle with the bottom out; and a horse cloth right over him with only his eyes left clear, and a pair of ears fastened on. He would rear and kick, and even run after people, and was the advance-guard going before the plough lads, entering the house before them, where the play was to be performed. The play was much like that given by the mummers.

At Cawston, in Norfolk, is preserved the Plough Light Gallery with its inscription: 'God spede the plow: and send us ale enow: our purpose for to make.' The plough, bedecked with many coloured ribbons, was taken into the church to be blessed and placed under the gallery.

This was really the first Feast of the year, being the first Monday after the Epiphany. In Cambridgeshire the labourers went round from house to house, cracking whips and calling as if to their plough-teams, seeking contributions from every householder. If these were not forthcoming they ploughed up the defaulter's doorstep. In two or three Cambridgeshire villages the ceremonial plough was still preserved, probably the old town or common plough. The ceremonies of the evening concluded by cutting a furrow before the farmer's door to signify that the Yuletide festivities were over, and the labourers ready to go forth to their work.

In Yorkshire, Rickers or Bones were played, together with a drum, whistle and concertina, by twenty young men dressed in white shirts covered with ribbons. They were harnessed to a Fond or Fool Plough, which ploughed up offending doorsteps. During the Feast the rickers kept time for the grotesque dances of Bessy and the Clown, and for the Sword Dance of the revellers.

On the Isle of Ely, the plough procession used to be accompanied by seven characters: The 'Humpty' who carried a hump, had a tail of plaited straw, horns, a black face, and a besom with which to persuade the unreasonable. The King and Queen, the latter being a man in woman's clothes; a Fiddler, a Purser to take charge of the contributions; and two men in high crowned hats, which were wound round with ribbons.

January 14th, Saint Hilary; the coldest day of the year.
January 21st, Saint Agnes; St. Agnes takes care of the lambs.
February 2nd, Candlemas Day:

> Where the wind is on Candlemas Day,
> There it will stick till the second of May.
> Candlemas Day,
>   Hussey goose lay:
> At Valentine,
>   Your goose and mine.

February 14th, Valentine's Day. On the eve of St. Valentine's Day, pin bay leaves to your pillow, one at each corner and one in the middle. You will then dream of your future lover, or the man you are to marry.

Valentine's Day was really a festival for the children, and several of their rhymes have been preserved. Grandmother's children were well to the fore on this day and knew many of these rhymes: Here is one in their idiom:

> The roses are red, the wiolets are blew,
> The pinks are sweet, and so are yew;
> If yew wull be mine, I will be thine,
> Sew its good mornin', Walentine!

And, of course, it was on this day that the birds mated:

> On St. Valentine
> All the birds in the air in couples do join.

Pancake Day was signalised in some instances locally by the ringing of the Pancake Bell at midday, but folks generally didn't know what it was for. Shrovetide really consisted of three days: Collop Monday, Pancake Tuesday and Fritters Wednesday. This was a season of free hospitality, and if anyone came in with the request: 'Please will yew giv'us a collop?' they were given a thick slice of ham or bacon, which they took home to cook.

> Knick knock, the pan's hot,
> We be come a-shrovin'!
> For a piece of pancake,
> For a piece of bacon;
> Or a piece of truckle cheese
> Of Dame's own makin'.

An ancient custom on this day was that of 'Thrashing the Fat Hen.' One of the labourers on the farm would be decked out with bells, and from his neck would be suspended a live fowl. Fellow labourers, who were blindfolded, were given branches with which to thrash him and the poor fowl, whom they followed by the noise. At the conclusion the fowl was boiled with bacon, and eaten with pancakes and fritters.

Shrove Tuesday was also the opening of the Shuttle-cock season for the children.

The Palm Cross was decorated with yew or willow on Palm Sunday and the choir halted there to sing. Rain water which fell on Holy Thursday or on Ascension Day, if caught and kept in a bottle, was a specific for sore eyes and cuts; besides it never stank however long it was kept.

Good Friday witnessed several customs, and the children had a rhyme for it:

> One for the poker,
> Two for the tongs;
> Three for the dust-pan,
> Hot Cross Buns!

And at one village the boys flew their kites on this day, from the top of what was called the Green Hill.

Many farmers would pay their men for this day, provided only they came to church. The payment was made in the churchyard after the service. This was observed in the next parish on the other side of the splash. Another curious and ancient custom, observed in an adjoining parish, was that of Keeping the Five Fridays in honour of the Five Wounds. One old lady there was noticed by a caller to be dressmaking on this day. When asked why she was not observing the occasion, she remarked it was of no use keeping one Friday if the other four were not kept also.

And, of course, there was the Good Friday Loaf, which had to be prepared and baked on the morning of that day. It was then hung up in the house and kept for a year, until the next was made. It was used medicinally, grated as required into water and given as a corrective for diarrhoea.

One should not forget the old custom of 'Lifting,' or 'Heaving' at Easter, when the womenfolk lifted the menfolk in a decorated chair, and vice versa, taking toll and exchanging kisses. In some parts, the children took coloured hard-boiled eggs to the top of a hill and rolled them down before eating them.

Mothering or Mid-Lent Sunday was the fourth Sunday in Lent:

> I'll to thee a simnell bring
> 'Gainst thou go'st a mothering;
> So that when He blesseth thee,
> Half that blessing thou'lt give me.

It was a custom in the one inn, 'The Ship,' of the old capital city across the purple heath from grandfather's home, to give its customers a biscuit to mumble with their beer. I think these were made on these old irons (one of which is still preserved in the museum there) and I suspect they were probably of monastic origin, as this was an old city of monasteries and churches, and the first see of the East Anglian bishops.

> A good deal of rain on Easter Day,
> Gives a crop of good corn, but little good hay.

'All Fools' Day,' according to the *English Dialect Dictionary*, is said to have originated from allowing insane persons to be at large on that day, while sane folks found sport in sending them on ridiculous errands.

> April with his hack and his bill,
> Plants a flower on every hill.

Moses Cook writing in 1675 said: 'December and January are the best times to fell Timber, but the oak in April if you would have the Bark, when the Moon is decreasing and the Wind not in the East.' This gave a clue to the harvests in my grandparents' county.

> Such a barksel, Such a haysel;
> Such a haysel, Such a harvest.

April 23rd is St. George's Day:

> When St. George growls in the sky
> Wind and storm are drawing nigh.

And as the children sang:

> Open the gates both wide and high,
> And let King George and I go by.

This was followed by St. Mark's Eve, when the church porch was watched at midnight to see who would die during the year, or suffer from a dangerous illness. Their apparitions were supposed to walk into the church at that hour; those who were to recover came out again; but those who were to die remained. It was also the Eve when young women could discover their future husbands, either by sowing hemp-seed in the garden at midnight, when they would be followed by their husbands-to-be in the act of mowing; or by baking a 'Dumb Cake,' when he would enter the room to turn it:

> An egg-shell full of salt,
> An egg-shell full of wheat meal,
> An egg-shell full of barley meal.

This was the practice in grandmother's county, but others place it at St. John's Eve.

> Maid who on the first of May
> Goeth afield at break of day;
> Wash thy face in dew off the hawthorn tree,
> And ever after a fair maid be.

May 1st was a great occasion, with celebrations local and general.

This was the day on which Jack-in-the-Green made his appearance, who was the sweep draped in green branch trappings attached to a wicker frame. And the children had a word for it:

> This is the day
> And here is our May,
> The finest ever seen.
> It is fit for the Queen,
> So pray, ma'am, give me a cup o' your cream!

Or this:

> First of May is garland day,
> Second of May is step-toe day:
> Knock at the knocker,
> Ring at the bell,
> Please for a penny for singing so well.

The May Branch cropped up again in the Horkey, which celebrated the end of the harvest. When the last sheaf had been duly cut and bound, the labourers stood round it and threw their sickles at it until they cut the band. Next, the last load of the harvest was piled on a cart and decorated with six May boughs, one at each corner and two lengthways in the middle. The labourers sat on the top as the load was drawn through the village, where the womenfolk came to their doors with pails of water. When the stacking was finished one of the branches was set before the farmer's door to suggest he should prepare the Horkey supper, and finally, the same branch was planted on the top of the last stack of harvest.

May 13th was observed as Midsummer Day by Sarah Self in grandmother's village. She would walk two miles to a certain field, wearing her pattens, and gather cowslips. These, she would make into a ball or balls, and on her return throw them over her cottage, reciting a rhyme.

May 14th, Pag-Rag Day, when servants would leave their places and 'pag' (pack) their clothes into white bags made for that purpose, and carry them home.

Whitsuntide was the season of many festivities and much village holidaymaking, with stalls on the Green, notably Broom's. Races were run in the Street, the distances being marked on certain trees. Hot halfpennies were thrown from the window of 'The Bell' by the landlord, and the antics of the children trying to pick up the hot coins were as funny as those of the monkeys at Gibraltar. The day usually ended with dancing, or stepping the shoe-jig at the pub, the men wearing high-heeled boots, beautifully made, for the occasion, lifting their heels and slapping the soles of their feet. But on St. Andrew's Day:

> The night is twice as long as the day.

June 24th. Midsummer Day; John Clare the Northamptonshire Peasant Poet tells of an old custom known as the Midsummer Cushion. This was a green turf cut and filled with field flowers, placed as an ornament in the cottages.

July 15th is St. Swithin's, which is still regarded with significance:

> Woe betide St. Swithin's bride!

July 25th. St. James the Great. Oysters come into season on Old St. James's Day, and old people believed that whoever ate them then would not lack for money during the rest of the year.

August 1st is Lammas Day, the ancient Feast of Thanksgiving for the first fruits of the corn.

August 24th is St. Bartholomew:

> All the tears St. Swithin can cry
> St. Bartlemy's mantle wipes dry.

September 29th. St. Michael's and All Angels, or Michaelmas Day, to be celebrated with a goose; it was also the great day of reckoning in the farmers' year:

> September, when by custom (right divine),
> Geese are ordain'd to bleed at Michael's shrine.

And if you did not baste the goose on that day, you would want money all the year. Blackberries from the bush must not be eaten after this day, as the devil has spat on them.

AN HOUR-GLASS ON THE RUN

November 11th. St. Martin's Day:

> On St. Martin's Day,
> Winter is on its way.

This used to be a day of feasting, in which geese and new wine took prominent part. On the ancient Clog Almanacs, this day is marked with a goose, because, as tradition states, St. Martin on being made bishop hid himself, but was found by a goose. It was the day also on which cows, oxen and swine were killed and cured for the coming winter, because of the lack of provender with which to maintain them:

> . . . dried flitches of smoked beeve,
> Hang'd on a writhen wythe since Martin's Eve.

Martinmas Beef was that dried in the chimney like bacon. It also gave rise to the saying:

> 'Its Martinmas will come, as it does to every hog.'

December 21st is St. Thomas's Day, when the old women went 'A Thomasin',' or collecting money. It was also known as 'Gooding' or 'Corning Day.'

Then comes Christmas Eve and Christmas Day. The traditional dish in grandmother's home and village on Christmas Day morning was frumenty; a concoction made of boiled wheat, eggs, sugar and spice. Egg-flip (eggs whipped up in brandy) was also drunk then. But:

> When Christmas comes in like a bride,
> With holly and ivy clad;
> Twelve days in the year,
> Much mirth and good cheer,
> In every household is had.

Yet:

> If Christmas on a Thursday be,
> A windy winter you shall see;
> Windy days in every week,
> Wintry weather strong and thick;
> Summer shall be good and dry,
> Corn and beasts shall multiply.

If the fruit trees are covered with snow on Christmas morning, they will be covered with fruit in the summer. Likewise, if there is sunshine on that day, it will be a good apple year. But:

> A light Christmas,
> A light harvest.

Boxing Day was also known as Offering Day.

This 'calendrical ritual' then, was something of the pattern of life that governed the year, abounding in bucolic fun and interest. Old customs survived from a remote past, adding spice to life in a quiet way. For instance, that of Dancing in the Hog Trough still existed and was quite common. It was occasioned by the marriage of the youngest child before the eldest. If this happened the latter had to dance in the hog-trough wearing green stockings. More often than not the old trough was danced to pieces, perhaps to the music of some rustic fiddler:

> When on't I plah—an' to't I sing,
> I makes the woods and walleys ring—
> An' fooks dew sah—though yeow ma' smile—
> Ta mah be hard amost a mile.

OLD CHRISTMAS

Lo, now is come the joyful'st feast!
   Let every man be jolly,
Eache roome with yvie leaves is drest,
   And every post with holly.
Now all our neighbours' chimneys smoke,
   And Christmas blocks are burning;
Their ovens they with bak't meats choke,
   And all their spits are turning.
   Without the door let sorrow lie,
   And if, for cold, it hap to die,
   We'll bury 't in a Christmas pye,
     And evermore be merry.
              George Wither *Juvenilia*

SOMETIMES there was no snow at Christmas and roses and geraniums bloomed in the garden, but at others the wind wailed through the leafless trees. Then a snow blast was driven against the windows—fine needle-point snow— and there was a sufficient fall in the temperature to bring it down. Then might come a thaw, just enough to give a fringe of icicles to the eaves, whereupon the frost returned, nipping and biting more viciously than ever. That was the time to visit grandmother's cheery and comfortable old-fashioned, low-ceilinged room, with the fire-shadows flickering to and fro. The huge logs crackled on the hearth, flames roared up the chimney and one felt it was Christmas and home. As grandmother felt the cold she always kept a good fire and scorned 'a hen's nose full,' as she termed it.

One or two very old people here and there, such as cousin Mary Godward, would only keep Christmas on the old day— January 6th. These old folk thought it was very wicked of them to have changed the calendar like that. After all, they said, 'our Lord won't ha' bin born twice!' Yet, as time moved on its way these old relations found themselves enjoying two festivals, since their pagan friends asked them out on December 25th, and they kept their own on January 6th.

Christmas had been always a great festival in grand-mother's home, but, of course, it was more than a day, since it was a cycle that lasted from Advent to Twelfth Night and like so much else in life it was honoured and enjoyed almost more in anticipation and preparation than in the day itself. It must be realised too, that grandmother's Christmas tree was not a pine or fir, but a holly tree. And surely she was right, with its enamelled leaves and jewelled fruit! She called it a *hulver*, and there was a Hulver Hill over by the Moor, and a hulver fence all round Quinton Wood's pightle on the Yoxford road.

This was the time when the village band came into its own, and went a-carolling about those quiet star-lit fields. One could hear them talking and laughing, now by the Yew Tree Corner, over by Title, and just faintly by the Packway. Anyone could have those pimping wood-wind instruments as far as grandfather was concerned, give him a bit of brass, and something whereon he could get the low notes. Grand-mother was none too pleased about these excursions, because the strong beer and home-made wines that were forth-coming at most of the calls needed a strong stomach and head. Although they set out with the best of intentions and could negotiate cart-tracks, stiles and field-paths without difficulty, yet as the night drew on to morning it was not surprising that some mistook the common path and fell into the mire.

> Rejoice, our Saviour he was born
> On Christmas day in the morning.

How pleasant it was as a child to lie in one of those truckle beds, in a room smelling of apples, and listen as the stars glistened and passed by.

When the family was young, Charlie and the girls would decorate the parlour with devices of their own making, hanging them about the windows, pictures and the fireplace.

Charlie would bring in one or two turnips which were cut in half and used as bases or stands for certain tree-like ornaments. First these half-turnips were coloured blue, then whin bushes or stalks were dipped in a pail of water and sprinkled all over with flour, and red berries stuck on the spikes. These fronds were then stuck into the rounded tops of the half-turnips and stood on the mantel-shelf, and anywhere else that afforded a ledge. They looked wonderful, although the flour-snow lacked the sparkle that Jack Frost usually applied.

On Christmas Eve the traditional dish of furmentory (frumenty) was prepared. The wheat to be stewed was placed in a long bag, and Charlie and Eliza catching hold at each end, using the bag as a chute, would throw the contents to one another, and beat it, so that the husks came away from the grain. To the prepared wheat was added a thickening of flour, and it was left for the night. At five o'clock the next morning Charlie got up, put the preparation in the boiler, and stirred it for nearly three hours lest it should burn. It was eaten off old wooden platters (heirlooms) at eight o'clock breakfast, sugar, spice and rum being added. Grandmother knew an old recipe for this, which ran:

'Take clean wheat and bray it in a mortar, that the hulk be all gone off, and seethe it till it burst, and take it up and let it cool; and take clean fresh broth, and sweet milk of almonds; and sweet milk of kine, and temper it all; and take the yolk of eggs. Boil it a little, and set it down and mess it forth, sweetened with rare sugar if it is to be taken by itself and not with fat venison or fresh mutton.'

Grandmother always excelled herself at the Christmas dinner. First, there was a hot mutton pie, with oyster patties, then a huge goose, one which had gobbled up many a tit-bit to hasten its own demise, with attendant vegetables. Ending up with a lemon pudding, plum porridge, junket, apple fritters. And should there be any room, a mince pie, baked in the old-fashioned coffin-shaped crust (learnt of her mother) to represent the cratch or manger in which the Holy Child was laid. What more would you, save a glass or two of harvest ale laced with gin, and drunk from tall glasses (like old champagne) kept by grandmother in the top part of her corner cupboard. Or, as an especial treat, one of the new sherry wine, the oil of which lingered lovingly on the old cut glasses. Or syllabubs made of whipped cream (whipped until the arm ached) and also served in tall glasses.

Games were played, some of which only came out on this day as hardy annuals. There was a game of dominoes, played with a set of hand-cut counters running up to double nines; and they were housed in a chip-carved box, a dug-out, the work of some old sailor on a long voyage. Being Methodists they did not go in for card games, other than those for children. These were Snap, Draw the Well Dry, Happy Families (a real joy, introducing the neighbours), and Twilight. Dr. Busby was another.

And then came tea, which was another feast to wait on digestion. Home sweet-pickled ham, wanmill cheese, home-made bread and butter, cakes and rusks, washed down with strong tea (Soochong flavoured with Pekoe, costing six shillings a pound) and cream in old Worcester noggins, looking like molten gold. But before tea, as was her daily custom, grandmother would drink a glass of cowslip wine.

Yes, they had good digestions in those days, and most of their alimentary troubles could be cured by generous doses of Epsom Salts or Jalap.

After tea they would gather round the fire and the box of Death Cards would be brought out, in memory of those who had been accustomed to take part in the family festival. Aunt Mahala, for instance:

> Afflictions sore long time she bore,
> Physicians were in vain.

And someone would begin to reminisce: 'Poor old Mahala, how she did enjoy a Christmas; but there she was ullus some untidy! You'd never think as how she'd got a frock to wear. And wasn't she always in a frap, muttering to herself while she was a busy cooking! Do you call to mind when she went to Frannigan Fair with her daughter Susan and come home with a new gown. That fairly stammed everyone.

'And wasn't she funny about them old coverlets o' hers; she said she had fifteen o' them, made by her poor old mother. I can hear her now: "They never have been used, an' never shall be in my time. No they 'on't!" '

As they went through the pack so each would come to life again—Ebenezer Woolnough:

> To all my friends I bid adieu,
> A more sudden death you never knew;
> As I was leading the old mare to drink,
> She kicked and killed me quick'n a wink!

Then—'Do you call to mind when Miss 'Lizabeth [Doughty] gave him a peach to take home to Riah [Mariah, his wife] who was ailing? She say, "I cooked that, an' I cooked it, but there, I never did think nawt on't! That didn't fare to eat wunnerful at all!".'

These having been conned over, lamented or laughed at, grandfather would develop an expansive mood and tell tales of his young days. When he was a boy the fear of Napoleon had not yet departed from the countryside. They expected him any hour. Grandfather would tell about precautions taken in the village, some being told-off to break down the brick ovens. (Had not the Little Corporal said that an Army marched on its stomach?) Others had to fell trees, while others had to remove any rolling stock, such as farm wagons, and assist the flight of the women and children into a safer place. Grandfather would point out the brick culvert he had ear-marked as a hiding-place for himself, as a very small boy.

Then there were the Fairs he had attended in his youth, small townships where the householders could brew and sell beer without a licence for two days and where they worked their own cider presses and sold the raw stuff for twopence a pint. Saxmundham had a Fair on Whit Tuesday, and another on August 18th for lambs. Some of the better-class folk used the genuine business stalls to replenish their stocks. For instance, one could buy Sheffield ware on one, and crockery ware at another, where a large stock of ewers and basins were laid out for inspection. But drinking was the order of the day—

> Rove not from Booth to Booth
> But Step in Here
> Nothing Excel [*sic*] the Music
> But the beer.

Another favourite drink on those occasions was 'Sugar and Done,' ordered by that name. It consisted of a pint of two-penny beer, and a half-pennyworth of sugar and nutmeg. Then there was 'Old Cow' which seemed to cause the road to fly up and strike one in the back! They used to say in those days—

> Nature for all abundant blessings sent
> Water for Swans:
> But beer for men was meant!

At one Lamb Fair they used to sell the lambs for a pound each, that is if they were good specimens, but poor ones went for as low as three for a guinea. Then there were stalls laden with legs of pork, tattooed with black pepper and all kinds of queer folk in charge of them.

Daniel Pettit, for instance, who was an incorrigible old

rascal. He ran a game called 'Three Pins,' at three cheeses a penny. One had to bowl an iron-bound ovoid wood along a plank to where three pins stood on a lozenge-shaped board. The game was to knock down the three pins three times in succession to score nine. But no one ever did so, save one, and he played as though by witchcraft. Daniel hated the sight of him.

When Daniel was hauled up before the magistrates for stealing the policeman's gloves (who was completely lost without them), he had the effrontery to say that he (the policeman) was worse than a kitten. Asked what he meant by that he replied, 'Well, sars, kittens are only blind for a few days, but ole Catchpole is ullus blind!'

They used to say that Daniel had enough brass in his face to make a copper and his one maxim was, 'Never venture your fingers between two eye teeth!' He came to die at last, his last words being, 'Put a bottle o' beer, and a new pipe and some bacca side o' me!' And his little old black pony and two dogs were shot and buried with him.

When grandfather was a boy, he with others would go round the village on St. Stephen's Day. They would catch a wren, kill it, and fasten it in the midst of a mass of holly and ivy on the top of a broomstick. Going from house to house, they sang

> The wren, the wren, the king of all birds,
> St. Stephen's Day was caught in the furze;
> Although he is little, his family is great—
> I pray you good landlady, give us a treat!

And so the day would draw to its close, but not before grandfather had been cozened into telling one of his ghost tales, which he could usually manage out of local lore.

'They used to tell of a man in our village who had a spirit come and sit by his bedside for three nights in succession;

and it never spoke a word! At the end of the third night it up and said, "Follow me!" Taking a spade the man and the spirit went about a mile away, over by Theberton, and the man was told to dig! Suddenly he unearthed a pot of gold! "My heart!" he exclaimed, and was just about to grab hold of that little lot, when the gold and the spirit vanished. Then he heard a sad whisper that the gold was not for him, but was intended for a grey-haired man not then born. (Why then did the spirit plague him with the sight of it?) Afterwards a child was born in the village with white hair, but no relation to him whatever, and when the child grew to manhood and followed the plough, he turned up the gold in that same spot. For he had hired himself to a man in Theberton.'

And so to bed, grandmother recalling in quiet memory her little boy who died one severe Christmas years ago and hoping that the robins would sing over his tiny grave in the little churchyard on Holy Innocents' Day.

> Ule! Ule!
> Three puddings in a pule;
> Crack nuts and cry ule!

RHYMING SIGNS

IF onc wanted further evidence of the happy life of the countryman in those early years of Victoria, it is forth-coming in the interesting signs which enlivened the homes and shops of some villages. They were common to many counties, although some were unique to the place and calling and they crop up here and there in the pages of old topo-graphical works. For the most part they were of wood, painted in Roman characters, on a white or black back-ground, with sometimes a coloured border. They must be looked upon today as the forerunners of advertising, and who indited them remains a mystery, often enough the tradesman concerned, but sometimes the schoolmaster or the writer of epitaphs.

The inn provided a good crop, exhibited internally and externally, a particularly fine specimen of the former being one of the puzzle variety, once to be found in the Broads district of Norfolk. The punctuation is thrown in to cause confusion. One can well imagine the amusement this caused amongst the old marshmen—that peculiar race—when any stranger appeared on the scene. It takes its place with the inscription on the stone which so puzzled Mr. Pickwick.

THEM ILL ERSLEA VET-HEMI!
LLT HEW HER RYME NLOW
ERTH EIRS-AILTH; EMA!LTS
TER SLE AVET-HE KI? LN,
FORAD-ROPO; FTH EWHI.
TESW ANA-LE-

Others to be found in prominent positions in inn parlours were:

RHYMING SIGNS

All you that stand before the fire,
To see you sit is my desire,
That others may (as well as you),
See the Fire and feel it too.

And this from Mulbarton, Norfolk—

Those that bring tobacco here
Must pay for pipe as well as beer:
And those who sit before the fire
Must move aside. For I desire
That all my friends, as well as you,
May see the fire and feel it too.

Then—

Since man to man is so unjust,
None can tell what man to trust;
I've trusted many to my sorrow;
Pay today and trust tomorrow.

The next is a fuller exercise and bears an introduction—

THE LANDLORD'S KIND CAUTION TO HIS CUSTOMERS.

Right welcome all who visit here,
I'll treat you with good wholesome cheer;
I deal in Ale, as crystal clear,
In Porter brown, and good strong Beer.
I've Rum and Gin, and Brandy too;
They suit myself and will please you.
My Wines would make a Nabob smile,·
My Whisky will your hearts beguile.
My Chairs are easy, Fires are bright,
So take a seat, yourselves delight.
My Tobacco's rich, Pipes white as snow,
Alike they're found to soothe your woe.

I'm ever ready to attend your call,
But I've no chalk to spoil my wall,
Chalk ever does sweet peace destroy,
Stirs up foul anger, stifles joy.
My liquors good, my dealing just,
My profits small, I cannot trust.
I'm sure these lines can cause no sorrow,
So pay today, I'll trust tomorrow.
If I refuse to trust a friend,
Or if I trust or money lend,
The one he takes it in disdain,
The other will my house refrain.

Here is an inn sign in the Suffolk idiom:

William Allen live here,
He sell spiritous liquors and good home brewed beer.

Here is another from Suffolk:

I, David Cranford, here attend,
For boots and shoes I've got to mend;
I nail them strong and mend them tight,
And ready money is my delight.

Then comes the barber, with this over a doorway at Bungay, Suffolk: and note the idiom:

Here lives William Pope, who shave for a Penny,
Walk in gents, you can't come to meany. [*sic*]

And this was once to be found at Framlingham:

Oh, Absolom! Oh, Absolom!
Oh, Absolom! My son,
If thou hadst worn a periwig,
Thou hadst not been undone!

But surely the best of all was at Beccles on the Waveney, rendered in the vernacular:

> All you who have hair and berds to crop,
> Just walk into my shavin' shop:
> Rich and luxorius I trim
> The roughest berds from any chin;
> I cuts the hair upon the newest plan,
> And charges littler than any man.

It might be mentioned that it was considered advisable to be early on a Saturday night for the weekly shave. Late comers were apt to feel very tender about their chins on leaving.

The importance attached to chimneys in grandfather's day is evidenced by the old Hearth Tax which, of course, had long since gone. The hearth was the centre of the home and through it evil spirits would make their attempts to enter the house. It is not surprising that more than one house-proud woman in grandfather's village would stuff with rags and paper any unused chimneys she might have, to keep out witches and imps. Is that what caused the chimney-sweep to sing? This is what Hissey has to say about one of these notices to be found in grandfather's locality:

'Yoxford is the name of this picturesque Suffolk village. Over the doorway of one of the rustic cottages here we read the following poetical effusion; is it the beauty of the spot, I wonder, that causes even the sweep to proclaim his trade in verse? Should not, however, a sweep know how to spell chimney? But perhaps this is a mere matter of detail. Here then is the verse:

> James Marjoram does live here,
> He sweeps the chimineys far and near;
> If your chiminey get on fire,
> He'll put it out at your desire.'

OLD ROMANCE

No more, no more, much honour aye betide
The lofty bridegroom, and the lovely bride;
That all of their succeeding days may say,
Each day appears like to a wedding day.

‹◇

GRANDFATHER'S village is situated some three miles inland, mid-way along the Suffolk coast. Moving southwards one comes to an old fortress, built in the time of the Stuarts, but well manned at the period of Napoleon's threat—Landguard Fort. Discharges by cannon at practice shoots could be heard in the village when the wind was favourable. Just at this point several waters meet, since the Orwell and the Stour run into the sea here; and across this confluence stands the harbour of Harwich. Both Landguard and Harwich figured in the Dutch Wars and it was hard by the former that the last landing of these intrepid assailants took place. Needless to say they did not stay very long or wreak much damage. Not far from Harwich is Dovercourt Bay, with an old squat church set on a village green. A quiet bit of old-world Essex.

As I have already mentioned, grandfather's childhood was spent under the scare of invasion, and all his childish fears were of 'Boney.' Before he was born, both the Suffolk and Essex coasts were manned by county militia, and a number of martello towers were built. Many of them still remain. They have taken on a certain picturesqueness, which could hardly have been apparent when they were rawly new. However, they served their day and that generation, and stand as crumbling memorials to the labours and fatigues of many a Company. Like all military occupations there must have been a lot of comings and goings, though these movements would by-pass grandfather's village, where they were merely concerned with the *status quo*.

OLD ROMANCE

In the course of the years, tour and tour about, there came a Company of the Loyal North Lincolnshire Militia to the same quiet Dovercourt recruited from Lincoln itself, and towns like Horncastle and Louth. Volunteers all of them, sons of business men, whose fathers had served in the regiment before them, finding something different from their ordinary daily routine. They came from the flat lands of Lincolnshire to the flat lands of Essex, so they found that much in common.

Amongst the number were two brothers, John and William Mason, having joined for the period of the war. They were of old yeoman stock, cattle graziers near Horncastle. The youthful John was of a sober, serious, religious turn of mind, evidently quartermaster to the regiment. Before being posted to Dovercourt he had been sorely wounded, not by French missiles, but by Cupid's darts. In other words, he had left a girl behind him. But not for long, for in the parish register of that same squat old church is the following entry:

'No. 142. John Mason of this parish, bachelor and belonging to R. North Lincoln Militia and Elizabeth Caborn of this parish spinster and belonging to the same Regiment were married in this church by Licence this seventh day of September in the year one thousand eight hundred and nine by me Wm. Whinfield, Cur. This marriage was solemnised between us.

John Mason.
Elizabeth Caborn.

In the presence of Wm. Mason.
Mary Wanash.'

And thereby hangs a tale, not quite the sort of rustic homespun chronicle that recorded the romances of grandfather's village, when they walked across the fields to church, walked back again to take part in a few junketings; and were at work the next day. No, this was something out of the 'sheres,'

with a background of comings and goings under a threat of
war, for at twenty-three Bessy was an old campaigner.

She had been attached to the colonel's lady (he was a
nobleman) from very early years, and had seen life in no
uncertain manner. She had travelled over most parts of
England, Scotland and Ireland in stirring times indeed. She
knew the alarm of sudden unexpected and immediate calls
upon the regiment to march to new stations; of stormy
crossings of the Irish Channel, when they were fastened
down under the hatchways, while the poor old ship plunged
and creaked, and they expected every minute to sink. Of the
seizure of baggage-wagons from enraged farmers; of the
overthrow of their carriages, and all kinds of odd adventures
on those old rutted roads.

Remembering the observation made to grandfather by
poor old Jimmy Elmey, concerning the superiority of the
dam over the sire, we might look a little more closely into
Bessy's origin. She came of a good family, born in the lovely
old wool town of Beverley, Yorkshire, and was baptised in
the ancient octagonal and curiously carved font of the
magnificent parish church of St. Mary's. A Caborn, named
from the village of that name, near Caistor in Lincolnshire,
home of her ancestors. Bessy was proud of her origin and the
place of her birth.

From the circumstances of the wedding you will conclude
that she met her husband whilst thus engaged; but it does
not appear to have been the case. One thing, however, seems
clear, she had learned to love a uniform as well as a man;
the shako, the tunic, the sword and the sash. Possibly tiring
of the adventurous life and a desire to be in the old sleepy
town again, had brought her back, and there she met her
lover. But they may have met before—who knows? He
appeared to be on terms of familiarity with her family.

And so they married, a quiet wedding, in that squat little
Essex church of All Saints, Dovercourt, so far from home,

and Bessy entered once again on a restless, trying life. But the questions arise, what did she wear? A poke-bonnet of straw or white beaver, trimmed with coquelicot ribbon; and somewhere about her a touch of Lincoln Green? How did she get there? By baggage convoy, diligence or stage coach? Her husband could, and did by virtue of his office, provide her with any available comforts; yet it was a case of here today and somewhere else tomorrow. Sometimes it was the Luddite malcontents in Lancashire, at others Irish insurrectionists. At last came the Peace of 1815, and on her advice, John resigned his commission. When the letter had been delivered to the post office, he returned saying: 'Now my soldier's life is ended!' and Bessy burst into tears.

What is a man to do? He reminded her that he had taken the step with her full consent and agreement; but Bessy was sad, not at the step taken, but from the memories of her somewhat stirring past, for though trying enough at times, it had been so full of grateful interest. At first they settled in Boston, but John had not entirely cut himself off from the regiment, for he was in some way still on the staff and the headquarters being at Lincoln, he found the journeys there irksome. So they settled down in the old cathedral city, to a large family such as was then common, and they were amongst the pioneers of Methodism in that place.

Great-grandmother Mason must have looked attractive in her poke-bonnet, ample skirt and shawl, and like grandmother Barham in her quiet village home was ever exercised in doing acts of charity. Bessy did not feel 'the luxury of doing good'—far from it; she did it from sheer goodness and kindness. Not content with giving, she visited the sick and poor, fearless of fever and the cholera that often raged; and no one came to her door in vain.

She died young, only fifty-one, and was buried in the south-west part of St. Mark's churchyard, where her father and eight of her own children had previously been interred.

With them she sleeps, where the guardian trees, as they yearly renew their glossy foliage, gently whisper among their young leaves of a coming resurrection.

Poor John, now disconsolate, was left to grow into an old, old man. He died in London and was taken back to lie beside his wife in his beloved Lincoln, the wife he had wedded as a soldier bridegroom, in the quiet little church of Dovercourt, before even Waterloo had been fought and won.

But what has all this to do with grandfather and grandmother? Just this, they had three daughters. Like other families in those days there were not always bacon flitches hanging in the chimney although there may have been a lot of hooks. There was but one opening for girls then, and that was Service. Besides, it was of no use whatever looking for last year's birds in that year's nest in any of those cottage homes. The two elder girls had sought to make a little livelihood. Eliza possessed a donkey named Mordecai, with which, harnessed to a little cart, they peddled sea-borne coal to widely separated doors. But Mordecai had a peculiar little trait in his character of sitting down in the road, if he objected to the load. And he would get up for no man, hence his name. How those girls laughed as they endeavoured to shift the load to suit his convenience, and coax him up again. However, that was a poor living and Eliza had perforce to part with her ass, not without sadness. Then a brilliant opening came her way, for in Yoxford was a large house where lived a Q.C. He had another house in the peaceful neighbourhood of Upper Norwood. It was so close to London, and the Crystal Palace had been newly removed there from Hyde Park. Moreover, the streets were lit by gas lamps! Here, at the foot of an extremely sharp rise, bearing in its name the mark of the countryside out of which it had been cut, Fox Hill, was as beautiful a place as any the district afforded. (Shades of pink coats, hessian boots and 'Gone Away!') And to a square-cut Victorian residence, called 'The Lions' (from two such animals of coade-stone set near the front door), came this simple Suffolk girl.

How did she come? First her box was made by the wheelwright, who made the coffins also and it was made like a coffin. A good square box with lock and key, covered in black cloth and studded with coffin nails. But it was not for an ending, rather for a beginning. Then grandfather harnessed the pony cart with the faithful Kitty, whom he was always enjoining to 'git up do!' meaning to trot, which she never did. And off they went to the station, the station all newly raw that he had watched being built. (He little thought then that it would see all his girls away.) Yes, there were tears, tears in the low-ceilinged room of fragrant memories and smell, and tears again, this time into grandfather's beard when the porter rang the hand-bell at the station, and the train drew away carrying that self-reliant young woman with her box in the van. Grandfather felt 'some bad' as he climbed into his lonely seat, and had not the courage to bid Kitty 'git up do!' So they ambled home to a strangely quiet old house.

But what of Eliza Ann? She was going into a new world, with all her worldly possessions in that box. The strangely shaped elms (*ellums* to her) seemed to fly past her barracky old third class compartment that was without a lid. It was a good job it was a fine day, but the smuts were horrid! They trundled past fields, farms, old houses, stopped at all the stations; and then dusty, dirty and tired drew into the smoke and rattle of Bishopsgate. That was bad enough, but it was only part of the journey, for still she had to get to 'The Lions' in Fox Hill. She felt the new home was well named, was it out of the *Pilgrim's Progress*? But there are more friends than foes in London, and the great bearded porters were wonderfully kind. They knew these young *mawthers* coming up from the country, whence they themselves had come; and since they were fathers they did their best to help. Anyhow, Eliza reached 'The Lions,' box and all, and when she went to sleep in her strange new bed, tucked away just under the slate roof, she cried quietly to herself. Now she had but one friend in the world, and that was her box, for when she lifted the lid it smelt of home. At the bottom was a little bit of butter, a few rusks, a tiny jar of honey, and a sprig or two of lavender. It was enough, and she felt brave again but she had no appetite.

Her work was hard, for there were more stairs in that small house than she had ever seen. She found herself under a not unkindly motherly cook, who ruled that well-scrubbed gleaming kitchen. Much of her life was lived almost underground, and then suddenly she was whisked off to sleep under the stars at the other extremity of the structure. Below were glistening covers, pot lids, a row of dangling bells, a round-faced clock, steel fender and black-leaded stove. Above, a bare apartment, and as hard a bed as could be found in any prison, a cane-bottomed chair, a washstand with ware, and her box. That was life at 'The Lions,' regulated by the pantry, and the constant motion of those bells. First one, then number two, then one and two together, something like the belfry at her old church, except they were so imperious and almost disagreeable in their wrangling.

Not much time off, but an occasional outing on an errand. It was indeed a foreign land, for when she went after a house-flannel and asked for a *dwile*, the man looked in astonishment. Besides he was not hairy like Broom, but bald and clean-shaven, and wore a white apron. 'Where have you come from, girl?' was his answer to the request; and it looked as though he thought she was one of those foreigners working at the Palace. She was glad to get out of his shop.

About the same time that Eliza landed at Bishopsgate with her box, came also to the Elysian heights of Upper Norwood a young lame man with a beard. He also had a box, securely fastened by lock and key and no one but himself ever opened it. He came from Lincoln, where he was born. His name was Edward Jacklin, son of a surgeon who had deserted his mother, and a grandson of Bessy. He had been apprenticed (his master's secrets to keep, etc.) seven long years to a Cordwainer, because of his disability, but that had degenerated into the office of cobbler. His young days had been a bit adventurous, more in the wars than his grandfather. He had fallen into the Witham near High Bridge, Lincoln, when fishing as a very little boy, but was happily fished out himself by a friendly dog. Then, joining with other boys in jumping off a heap of stones whilst at play he dislocated his knee-cap. That should have been no great matter, but most unfortunately for him he got into the hands of a so-called doctor (not his father), was taken home, placed on the kitchen table, his knee cut about without the use of any anaesthetics and lamed for life.

Eliza was seldom allowed out, yet she had every other Sunday off, and went to chapel. Edward was also sober and religious, like his soldier grandfather, and he too went to chapel. And so they met, two lonely souls in a strange land, fell in love and married. She with her bright eyes, dark long hair, trim appearance and sturdy character. (Had not the butcher's boy realised she was not to be trifled with when his ears were boxed?) He with a crooked leg, handsome beard and long pliant hands. It was almost as quiet and hurried a wedding as the one at Dovercourt.

Then home, to a little narrow tall house, set in a row, along a street which bore the name of St. Hugh. Was not that little martyr saint the patron of that Minster set on a hill, under the shadow of which Edward was born? Yet, it was its only claim to sainthood, for it was a street on an incline, dominated by an immense gin-palace at the top and trailing off into a mission church at the other end. A clear case of 'Pull devil, pull baker!' And the children played tig about the gas lamps.

Here the people sang *Rule Britannia* and got beautifully drunk on beer at a penny a pint. And pauper funerals gave a poor life an inglorious end, as they rammed the old coffin under the rusty hammer cloth, and jigged up the one horse into a trot; and the little white coffins too often followed after. And street-hawkers sang their wares—'Fine l–a–a–rge SHRIMPS!' The muffin man with his bell could be heard coming nearer and nearer, and then fading into the distance. The lavender sellers also, with the perfectly pitched deep rich contralto of the ostrich-feathered, ear-ringed woman, and fine baritone of her pearly-coated companion. They would sing with the left hand cupped below the cheek to give the echo. And who could resist it?

> Will you buy my sweet blooming lavender?
> There's your sixteen dark blue bunches a penny
>   All in full bloom!
> You buy it once, you will buy it twice;
> It will make your linen clothes smell sweet and nice.
> Come all you young ladies and make no delay,
> I gathered my sweet lavender, and am round once a day.

The house backed on to a railway station. And among the trains that were belled away, there were certain blue engines with stove-pipe funnels. They no longer ran from Bishopsgate, but from Liverpool Street to Croydon and back again. There was a certain magic in those particular blue engines to Eliza for they puffed the way home. Home to her cowslip fields, coloured hedgerows, waving corn, to mother now grown so old, to father with his fustian clothes, rubicund face and horny hands. And it was one of those engines that took her to have her first baby, in the little apple-smelling room that once was hers.

16 12